MW01008897

GYPSY
SIBELLA COURT

Interior photography by Chris Court
Travel photography by Sibella Court

HARPER
DESIGN
An Imprint of HarperCollinsPublishers

CONTENTS

A world of colour

I like to look at life in colour. It's a strong memory trigger and, for those of us with poor memories, a gentle reminder is always welcome. To me, everything is about colour. I want this book to reveal its importance, power and ability to transport you to places you've been to or want to go to. Coming from a styling background, colour has always been the most important tool with which I work. It has led me to create my own paint range based on my 10-colour palette theory, as well as many commercial interior spaces, styled sets for magazines and other product ranges. This is tried & tested – I use it every day!

As a way of looking at the world, colour can be both captivating and appealingly abstract. In my years as a stylist, I developed a 10-colour palette theory that gives me very clear boundaries to work within and has turned out to be the best starting point for decorating any space. I may only use a few of those colours at any one time or in a particular space, but having the palette there allows me to experiment and play with the feel of the space. I know that as long as I keep within the palette, the end result will have a sense of clarity to it.

I believe places reveal their identity through a colour palette, and in this book I have created one for each country I visited. I look for colour combinations in the local architecture, crafts, textiles, buildings, nature, art, food, even transport (may that be a camel, train, tuktuk or rickshaw) – anything really, and you can see this when you look at my travel photography throughout these pages. Don't get overwhelmed by this idea; it can be as simple or as complex as you like. In Scotland, the palette revealed itself honestly through the constancy of the highland landscapes, whereas in Turkey, it came to me in a moment. I wandered past a shoe-shiner toiling by the Aegean Sea and his wares scattered on a table presented the entire palette.

When you are travelling, take note of what's around you – don't set out to find, but to discover. I take a lot of photos (and many notes) that get edited into the story you see within these pages. Keep in mind that places may have different palettes depending on the season, and you might come up with something very different to mine depending on your adventures and your way of seeing the world. The palette may not be obvious to you at the time; it may only be when you're looking back at your photos or simply reminiscing that it reveals itself. There are no rules – I simply offer guidelines & some ideas to inspire.

Something I find very useful, once home, is to look at my photos and pull together a colour box. It might not necessarily contain possessions I collected in that country – in fact, it often doesn't – but using inspiration from the photos, I gather together objects, fragments, flotsam & jetsam. These might be pieces of fabric, ribbon or other materials, beads, matchbooks, napkins from a restaurant, a glass evil eye, a feather or a leaf. I add to, and subtract from, that collection until I create the colour palette.

Note: There is a Pantone app you can use that pulls a five-way colour palette from a photo for you – an easy, fun way to record a palette on the go.

Making colours

I've known Charly Wrencher since I was 16 – he was the only good-looking boy at Marist Brothers. We rekindled our friendship years later, and I've been spending time with him and his wife, Jane, at their lovely house & studio in Possum Creek.

Charly paints in oils to look like watercolours, and makes all his own colours, using ochres, charcoal and other pigments mixed with oils, to get exactly what he wants. He's very influenced by his environment, usually using where he lives as the subject of his work, and there are many layers in his paintings.

He and I have a similar passion for colour, so he was the obvious person to work with me on the palettes for *Gypsy*.

I sent him travel pics and colour boxes to get him started. I left Charly with these to see what palettes he'd come up with, and then finessed them with him once I'd finalised the interior shots I was using in the book.

I loved sitting with him as he was mixing the paint – it reminded me of *The Craftman's Handbook*, a book I came across when I was studying 14th-century Italian art. It was written by Cennino d'Andrea Cennini, an artist in jail, who revealed all his recipes for making colour.

The palettes in this book will be added to my current 110-colour paint range. Available as a palette or individually, the colours have been matched and mixed to perfection so that you can harness *Gypsy* as you create your own colour scheme at home or in a commercial space.

Storytelling

I use history as a reference point for many of my travels, as well as the interiors I style & design. Maybe my love of research sparks this. I like the type of research journey that leads you to something unexpected, a kink in the road that can be saved up for later if it appears irrelevant for now.

Quite a few years ago, I read Rebecca Stott's *Darwin and the Barnacle*, which talked of Charles Darwin first foraging for specimens off the Firth of Forth when he was a student at the University of Edinburgh. This put Edinburgh on the map for me and was enough of an excuse to head in that direction.

In many interiors or houses, there is a mix & layering of periods, styles, tastes & generations (unless you are a purist): it might be heirlooms from times gone by, a roadside find, hand-me-downs or gifts, a modern fad, original features used in a building's structure, even a past DIY folly or the debris of family life.

You can use your own travel history & memories in the same way. It's not about shipping furniture & props home (although this is lovely if you can! And a cheaper way to go rather than getting busted for excess luggage at the airport), but about reminders of your travels that can be incorporated into your existing interior. You can use everything you already own, but simply rearrange and edit it in a different way. This can be in the form of translating an observation, colour combination, planting, texture, finish, even window treatments & furniture placement.

You can edit each layer in different ways to express specific things at different times, then change them up to change the story of the space – no interior is permanent.

I styled every single shot in this book specifically to demonstrate this process. Many objects in the shots are my own pieces that I've been given or have picked up from faraway places, mixed in with products from all the fabulous shop owners, artists and designers I know who have lent me their wares to shoot for *Gypsy* in amazing locations around Australia. These people are my best-kept secrets and have now become a part of my story and, in the back of book, I share how wonderful and special they are and provide an insight into their own stories.

Let your house be a place to tell stories. By surrounding yourself with objects & translations of your very own travel observations, you create a place full of your memories; a unique, authentic space that reflects your personality. This, for me, is captured in the word 'palimpsest'. It is the lives lived in a house that makes it a home.

Palimpsest: the ghost of what once was, the memory of times & people gone by in an object; its history & past use.

Spinning the globe

I like to come up with reasons for wanting to visit a place. I save them up & add to them. Once a place goes on my 'list', I might get a book recommended or stumble upon an obscure museum; a fabric I like might have been woven there; or the origins of an alcohol or a maker's history of a piece of furniture might intrigue me. As I collect this information, different destinations jostle for a position in the Top 5.

The choice might end up being as simple as, 'While I'm in the vicinity, it would be rude not to pop in.' When you live as far away as I do in Australia, no trip has a single reason for travelling. While I may appear to be gallivanting around the world, I might combine a holiday with a book chapter, a fair, some product development or an editorial shoot.

When I have chosen one destination, I find it best to pull out the atlas and see what is in the surrounding areas. For example, on the Scotland trip to research for *Gypsy*, I flew into London and stayed for a dinner with my UK publishers before heading down to Charleston Farmhouse near Lewes, formerly owned by the Bloomsbury Group and top of my list for an age. Then over to Hastings to stay the night with my amazing friend Alastair Hendy, owner of A G Hendy Home Store and resident of the most amazing 15th-century Tudor house, before catching the train to pick up my father and begin adventures in Edinburgh. Take an extra day to see something wonderful!

As a lover of maps, I see in them the opportunities to tick things off my list. I pore over old maps and cartography and see where the country boundaries used to lie and how they have changed. Indochine and Transylvania are no longer referred to by those names, but therein lies romance and that is the romance I travel with!

Look for maps in different languages, ones that are hand-drawn, second-hand, found in markets or by the way.

Wayfaring companions

I travel with many different companions, as well as on my own. I like that this can determine the structure of a journey.

I embrace the 'constraints' that come from travelling with different people: it might be that I tag along for the ride on someone else's trip. It could be full of visiting artists, markets, furniture makers and fairs, as I do on Anthropologie's home design team inspiration trips. With roadtrip companions, the lunches & dinners get longer, the pace slows somewhat and the scapes become bigger as more land is traversed. These companions create a common story, a shared memory, and influence the way I think about the place and the trip.

When I am by myself, I follow my own agenda: usually a jam-packed itinerary of historical houses, markets, cafes & bars, walking, shopping, artists' studios, collections, trades & makers, loosely structured around early starts, writing & editing the day's photos. My motto for photographs is 'Keep the best, chuck out the rest.' I believe the first impressions of a place are so important: there's an excitement that comes from a brand new place. I try to take lots of photos upon arrival with these fresh eyes.

I like to shake up my companions within one trip, spending just the right amount of time before changing countries & meeting my next adventure or seeking out on my own. For this book I travelled many, many miles meeting with friends from across the globe via sailboats, trains, planes, tuktuks, taxis, motorcycles, one horse & cart, cars with drivers, cars that I drove, cars that went on ferries and ferries alone, puddlehoppers, bicycles, and a vintage Mercedes. Not to mention the steps I walked, ran, climbed and hiked. These paths I trod and traversed, and the tales uncovered along the way, are revealed in these pages, perhaps indirectly, and even though you weren't there, they'll hopefully inspire you to make your own adventures and create your own stories.

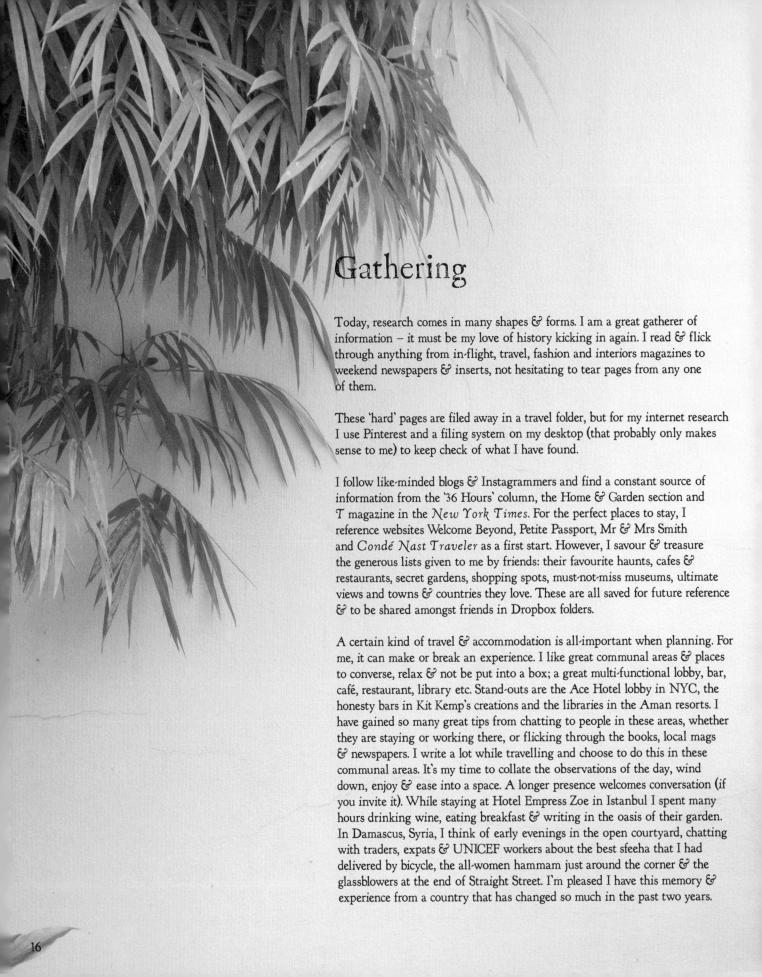

Gathering

Today, research comes in many shapes & forms. I am a great gatherer of information – it must be my love of history kicking in again. I read & flick through anything from in-flight, travel, fashion and interiors magazines to weekend newspapers & inserts, not hesitating to tear pages from any one of them.

These 'hard' pages are filed away in a travel folder, but for my internet research I use Pinterest and a filing system on my desktop (that probably only makes sense to me) to keep check of what I have found.

I follow like-minded blogs & Instagrammers and find a constant source of information from the '36 Hours' column, the Home & Garden section and T magazine in the *New York Times*. For the perfect places to stay, I reference websites Welcome Beyond, Petite Passport, Mr & Mrs Smith and *Condé Nast Traveler* as a first start. However, I savour & treasure the generous lists given to me by friends: their favourite haunts, cafes & restaurants, secret gardens, shopping spots, must-not-miss museums, ultimate views and towns & countries they love. These are all saved for future reference & to be shared amongst friends in Dropbox folders.

A certain kind of travel & accommodation is all-important when planning. For me, it can make or break an experience. I like great communal areas & places to converse, relax & not be put into a box; a great multi-functional lobby, bar, café, restaurant, library etc. Stand-outs are the Ace Hotel lobby in NYC, the honesty bars in Kit Kemp's creations and the libraries in the Aman resorts. I have gained so many great tips from chatting to people in these areas, whether they are staying or working there, or flicking through the books, local mags & newspapers. I write a lot while travelling and choose to do this in these communal areas. It's my time to collate the observations of the day, wind down, enjoy & ease into a space. A longer presence welcomes conversation (if you invite it). While staying at Hotel Empress Zoe in Istanbul I spent many hours drinking wine, eating breakfast & writing in the oasis of their garden. In Damascus, Syria, I think of early evenings in the open courtyard, chatting with traders, expats & UNICEF workers about the best sfeeha that I had delivered by bicycle, the all-women hammam just around the corner & the glassblowers at the end of Straight Street. I'm pleased I have this memory & experience from a country that has changed so much in the past two years.

I might choose hotels based on the architecture or history, a designer who inspires me, or the simplicity of a local place. You might find me staying in a yurt overlooking the Aral Sea, a resort in the rice fields, a yacht in the Mediterranean, a humble B&B in the highlands or a fabric tent in the desert. I am not always successful, but if uncomfortable, I have no hesitation in finding somewhere more in tune with what I desire.

I know all the new technologies, applications and social media platforms might not hold the romance of slow travel to far-flung places from another time, but use what you need to help you store & gather the information you find, in order to have the travels you dream of.

I am

I am a historian
I am a bowerbird, nomad, stylist,
etcetera
I am a designer of bars, restaurants
& hotels
I am The Society inc.
I am a maker of products
I am a trickster & attendant of
speakeasies
I am a lover of the remnants that
get left behind
I am a globetrotter
I am a user of ahoy & writer of
dictionaries
I am part pirate
I am a collector of specialised
tradesmen
I see in colour palettes
I write in brown paper journals
I travel with my imagination &
with aeroplanes
I am having a break from books
after this one

Scent & soundscapes

Every place I visit has its own scent: usually a layering of scents that create pure romance and transport you back to your gallivants.

I believe in this so much that I have created my own soap range based on the scents from the countries I visited for my book *Nomad: Bringing your travels home*.

I like to plan my adventures around the seasons. Although this is not always possible, it gives you a good reason to revisit a place on another occasion. When I visited Transylvania, I was two weeks shy of wildflower season. Hiking through the mountains, we saw some tiny early orchids and hellebores, and it was spongy underfoot with tendrils, buds & growth. I could only imagine the nature show I missed out on.

The scent was layered with almond blossom, the first spring shoots, honey and heady lilac, with a distant smokiness of the charcoal burners. It's important to remember that a trip during another season would create an entirely different scent altogether.

In Indochine, it was a combination of incense burning at the temples, refreshing lemongrass-scented cloths handed to us on arrival at Amansara, the sticky rice for alms housed in soft woven bamboo containers and lotus petals floating in large clay pots of fresh water.

In Scotland, the scents were grassy & mossy, thick with mist & water as we drove through tree-lined roads lochside, with hints of heather & wild thyme as the scapes opened to the wild western shores.

You can create layers that satisfy different senses, and give your interiors depth, dense with memories & stories. Consider a scent as much of a souvenir as an object.

I feel the same way about soundscapes and believe this is a sense that often goes unnoticed. When I am creating a commercial space, I have to consider soft and hard surfaces and how these will control noise levels and allow sound, even footfalls, to be absorbed or not absorbed. This is just a part of my fascination with soundscapes and foley (reproduced sound).

I met a German photographer, Hans Georg Berger, in Laos who spends a lot of time with different religious communities around the world. He had been going to Luang Prabang in the late '70s & early '80s before it was open and you had to have a very official letter for permission to visit. The only way to get in was by elephant or archaic, unreliable Russian planes that were not delayed by hours, but by days. Due to these restrictions, very few people visited and the only noise of traffic was the shuffle of sandals flip-flopping on the ground. Even though it was not my experience, it appealed to my sense of romance and this is the soundscape of Indochine for me.

At Timberyard, a restaurant in Edinburgh, the owner asked me what I thought of the soundscape in the bathroom. It was a recording of one of their favourite winemakers in Italy, making all his wine by hand.

For a lot of people, music can be a useful way of instantly evoking a time and a place. The sounds that affect me, though, are more the sounds of the street, the ambient sounds around me. I'll never forget the very first time I heard the call to prayer in the early morning from my hotel room in Istanbul or, when I was with my dad in San Francisco, the plaintive tones of a lone clarinettist busking on a dark and empty Union Square.

There are things that you can't necessarily see, but you can hear, smell and feel them and they are memories of all the things you love. These are what make a space special and personal.

Gallivanting with a purpose

I recently stumbled upon the word 'vagabonding' and it hit home. I discovered a perfect definition for it when I was reading *The Hare with Amber Eyes*. It describes vagabonding as appearing to be 'recreational rather than diligent or professional'. An activity that gets 'the pleasure of the searching right, the way you lose your sense of time when you are researching, are pulled on by whims as much as by intent'. This seems to encompass all that I do while travelling or determining my destination and researching for my adventures.

I like to have things to do as well. It is not a rigid itinerary to be kept to; it just gives me a loose guide that so often leads to other exciting things. I do not hesitate to contact places, people, shops, museums or libraries of interest to make an arrangement to call in or check on access, opening times or special request visits. My mum taught me this; before then, I had never thought that I was allowed in such places. If you are interested and passionate (it never hurts to use research as an excuse and always remember to give plenty of notice), most people from these cultural institutions and the like will grant you access.

For my interior styling work, I keep up to date & in contact with artists, furniture designers & other interesting people by visiting furniture & art fairs. These happen at certain times of the year in different countries and are always fun, full of energy & accompanied by satellite shows, pop-up restaurants, shops & other goings-on around town. You might find me in Milan for Salone Internazionale del Mobile, Eindhoven for Dutch Design Week, New York for the International Contemporary Furniture Fair, Paris for Maison et Objet or Ho Chi Minh City for the local furniture fair.

Being a reader and a lover of books, I've timed a couple of visits to India to coincide with a side trip to the Jaipur Literature Festival – depending on who's on the programme, it can also satisfy a lot of my other interests, and lead me towards new & unexpected ones.

As a great market goer, I search for local, daily, food, flea, seasonal & antique markets wherever I am. I have been known to book a trip just to get to a market: one of my favourites is the Foire Nationale à la Brocante et aux Jambons held outside Paris in March and September.

GALAPAGOS

&

ECUADOR

Isla Bartolome

Isla Santa Cruz

Isla Isabela

P a c i f i c

LINEA EQUATORIAL

flamingo
hummingbird
sandpiper

Names of roses

butterfly   don juan
gypsy boy   fortune teller
moody blue
magic carpet
evening star
apothecary's
celeste

magenta crush
violetta
alpina

alizarin (crimson)
ink

Galapagos & Ecuador

My Ecuadorian journey started in Quito, the highest capital in the world, a city of softly painted buildings in an array of taffy colours & old-fashioned shops: candlemakers, bakers, church suppliers, tailors, men's stores. I stumbled upon a haberdashery where the spools of cotton, beads, zippers and scissors were all in custom-made cabinets in a horseshoe arrangement, lots of little glass-fronted drawers showing off their colourful contents & an old-fashioned cashier station overseeing all proceedings. Rugged up and with my trusty panama, I was eager to explore the highlands for horses, llamas, alpacas & rose farms – I used to find their harvest at the flower markets in NYC. In some ways, it was the very simple desire to know the source of the things I buy that led me to Ecuador.

Heading through the Andes on steep and winding roads towards Hacienda San Agustin, rocky sharp mountains stretch for the skies on either side. We pass cobblestoned towns with traditionally dressed women, gossiping streetside, in deep green-on-green layers of fringed shawls, heavily pleated wool skirts, stockings and felted feathered hats in jewel tones.

Flowers are abundant, spilling from pots of all sizes & finishes on the wraparound verandahs of the haciendas, in windows & rambling gardens; the vibrancy of poppies in the misty deep green mountains, the pinks & magentas of ancient geraniums while hummingbirds with iridescent blue feathers flit at great speed. A visit to a rose farm reveals every variety in every colour destined for faraway markets; all long stemmed & Valentine's Day perfect.

At first it was hard to see how the colours of the chilly mountains of Ecuador would come together with the equatorial, rocky and, in parts, surprisingly barren islands of the Galapagos. Working boats painted as blue and green as the ocean had bumpers of intricately hand-knotted blue rope. Although it wasn't flamingo season, we came across a lost flock, all soft pink from their diet of shrimp and algae.

I found that, in some ways, the Galapagos and Ecuadorian landscapes offered the same colours but showed them off in very different ways – a fabulous styling technique from nature itself. I considered whether to even place these two distinct places together, but if a trip is planned to one, it would be foolish not to explore the other. For these reasons, your inspirations are likely to come home all mixed up & this is very natural.

In a remote cove of pink sands, the shores are strewn with sea turtle tracks, sea urchin quills & coral fragments, with the dunes behind speckled with bluey-green prickly pears & the holy trees that lend a beautiful scent to the scape. It was all very David Attenborough, and it became clear to me how this part of my gypsy roving fitted together as I watched blue-footed boobies dance, saw the aquamarine, turquoise & milky greens of the sea and the shock of orange & red Sally Lightfoot crabs scuttling across the cool coral sand.

hacienda

flamingo

sally lightfoot

alpaca

isola

booby

flotsam

hummingbird

st anthony

sea lion

Inspiration from a trip will never be translated in the few mementos you bring back (unless you did some serious posting home) – and shouldn't be! Gather paraphernalia that reminds you of an area and mishmash it together. High up in the Ecuadorian mountains, the homes were comfortable, with interiors that spoke of family history, each piece a memory but not hodgepodge. Make it a beautifully orchestrated journey throughout your house or apartment, including the transitional and forgotten spaces.

Don't be afraid of colour. It doesn't necessarily mean bright or overwhelming. Here it has become its own neutral – a beautiful base to build the rest of your room around. It reminds me of driving very high up into the clouds, surrounded by vivid green fields & mountains.

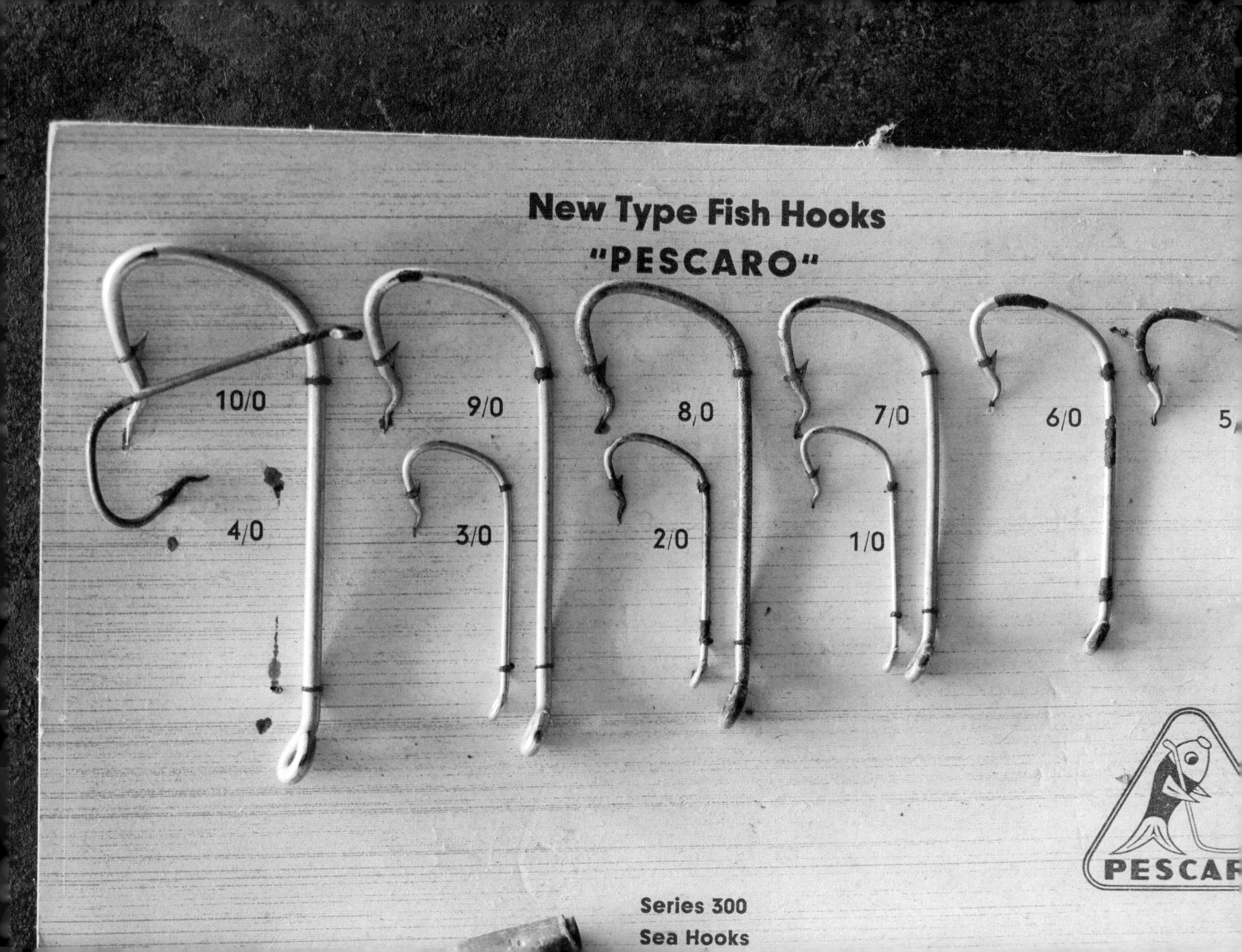

New Type Fish Hooks
"PESCARO"

10/0

4/0

9/0

3/0

8/0

2/0

7/0

1/0

6/0

5

Series 300
Sea Hooks

PESCAR

The Galapagos Islands were full of
penguins, blue-footed boobies, marine
iguanas & all the wild creatures
sailors would have seen on their
travels many years ago. The beauty &
marvel of the place is the proximity
of the animals: close enough to reach
out & touch them! It is as if you
could stand on your tippy-toes and
tickle the feathered chests of the birds
that hover above your head.

One morning we set off to a deserted
cove to go snorkelling. The walk
there was along a beautiful wooden
boardwalk through mangroves with
orchids and other air plants growing
amongst them, hanging down and
interwined through the scape,
much like the potted plants in this
space, tendrils falling to the ground.
Magical. On the beach and rocks of
piratical cragginess, caramel velvet
sea lions sunned themselves amongst
stones that could be Brancusi,
Noguchi or Hepworth sculptures –
the perfect natural shape for them
to while away the afternoon, rolling
& tumbling on the water's edge and
swimming playfully amongst us. We
were only distracted by the most
graceful (& very large) sea tortoise
cruising by. A dip-dyed curtain in
watery tones, changing like the
colour of the sea as the tide goes out,
and a hexagonal-patterned runner,
reminiscent of the tortoise's shell,
complete this interior.

As a nature sanctuary, nothing can come in or go from the Galapagos Islands. I bought this collection, put together in the '60s by a fisherman's wife who lived on the part of the Moruya River where the river meets the sea south of Batemans Bay, NSW. I put them on table surfaces to be arranged by size, colour, shape or whatever I desire. Not to be shut away behind glass as it is a lovely experience to hold them.

Embrace unusual spaces. This was a very narrow and what many would see as quite an awkward space. Rather than being scared of small spaces, make them inviting and intimate – like the quarters of a ship's captain! One night in the Galapagos, I dined at the Cave. A building of lavastone, white-washed and with the feel of a captain's nook: round windows, a low ceiling, fireplace, positioned on the water (arrival is via water taxi) and with a welcome of rope doormats. You could imagine it being built when visitors were few. Caramel & cream stingrays were feasting at the bottom of the stone stairs.

Let the space direct you instead of the other way around. Often you will create something you never would have thought of. The Galapagos was a stopping point for merchants, buccaneers, specimen collectors, explorers and whoever else was lurking in the waters. Here, they'd stock up on tortoise meat, which would last for six months and guard against scurvy. Some of the first things that attracted me to these islands were the stories of the trade winds, of seafaring exploration and the romance of Darwin's discoveries here.

[NEXT PAGES] In Quito, I went to Casa Museo Guayasamin, a museum which houses famous Ecuadorian artist Oswaldo Guayasamin's studio and his home, which had a wall of nooks with hanging ship's bells. A wall can be a cupboard, window or screen, textured, of unusual shape and three-dimensional. Embrace any unusual backgrounds and let them guide your display.

Here sits a casual setting on the table for what will be the beginnings of a long lunch. The mix of textures shows off vintage and new cushions as well as a beautiful blanket as a make-do tablecloth. This gives the feeling that everything is handcrafted, although it is not – the fact that it is a little off and not quite perfect is the reason why the scene is pulled together. By creating a casual setting, your guests will feel comfortable and your gathering or event will be guided accordingly. A styled interior should not be seen as simply something to admire from the outside, but must be appropriate to live in and be a part of; it should act as a foundation to create stories upon that reflect your life and become a part of your memories. I would eat a dessert of passionfruit pie, chocolate cake and fig with cheese in syrup here with good friends over many hours, as I did in an Inca stone dining room what feels like many moons ago.

In Quito, there are all these beautiful churches – one of my favourites was La Compania, with the most incredibly detailed stonework. Like any South American city influenced by the Spanish, Quito is very Catholic, so you discover shrines all over the place. Other towns have the typical church square with all the main buildings surrounding it. Here I have created a little make-your-own altar. Mine is a tribute to travel, where every cross could be a representation of a place or trip – I have included a fun one from Byron Bay to reflect my location. You can pick up crosses anywhere and, if you dig a little deeper, they come with a story or the history of the town or country you're in. In an antique shop I saw a figure of Saint Anthony, and through my enquiries discovered that if you have lost something or are lacking in love you pray to him (for love, place his image facedown under the pillow).

Some people collect magnets (which I'm not encouraging) or postcards, make your collection personal and aesthetically pleasing so you can show it off for guests once home, and have as a reminder for you. A travel shrine. Hung by the bed, they can also protect you while you're sleeping and ward off bad dreams. I like the way magic realism and superstition are a part of religion in South America. I personally pick up textiles all over the world because they pack flat and travel easily – don't be shy to change them regularly, it transforms your room through a colour palette.

[PREVIOUS PAGES] I am obsessed with flamingos. They dance in the water! Their whole body movement is absolutely mesmerising. I felt so lucky to see a flock out of season. In my mind they deserved to be blown up in a space – giant! Don't be scared of overdoing it – sometimes you just might pull it off. If you don't, it doesn't matter because interiors are temporary and having fun with a space is much more satisfying than vying for perfection all the time. It is the imperfections that make it personal and interesting. Designer Marion Hall Best has been an inspiration to me in the way I've put colour together here – she would tone down colour blocks by using natural flooring. It's all about balance. Lean art on the floor and hang sheets of wallpaper so they are easy to move around and be restyled or packed away (perhaps when your flamingo obsession passes – ready to be revisited next time).

[THESE PAGES] I could never overestimate the importance of freshly cut flowers – all the better if they're home grown. In the haciendas throughout Ecuador, roses & geraniums are in every room. It's a nice little surprise when there are flowers somewhere unexpected like your bathroom. Attention to detail is important when creating a space, as it is those small moments that make it memorable. I love picking up salvaged bathroom fixtures – this sink is the ultimate powder-room size, petite and elegant with lots of history. I recently renovated my own bathroom and mixed old & new fixtures to give it plenty of layers and interesting patina – not just shiny & new. My own sink is an old Parisian cleaner's sink and the taps are from Porte de Clignancourt in Paris, a convenient accident.

Animals spotted in
Galapagos

Sea Lions
Blue-footed boobies
Pelicans
Sally lightfoot Crabs
Orcas
Pufferfish
Marine Iguana
Hummingbirds
Golden Finches
Puffins

This is the meeting of the mountains & the sea. Up in the
mountains, there were rose farms and all of the haciendas were
surrounded by beautiful gardens. The hacienda I stayed in was very
high up, and it got darker & moodier along the cobblestoned village
roads as we drove past shepherds and schoolchildren throwing stones
into the river, while our driver checked with local men & women for
directions. Owned & built by an Ecuadorian president, the hacienda
continues to be run by the same family and sits on 40 hectares. They
run horses, a cheese factory and a B&B. The rooms were filled with
antiques discarded from the family's other dwellings (just like any
holiday house) – but here they were hand-carved, heavy and robust.
There were bentwoods as well, which, to me, are casual and belong
at the seaside, bringing the elements of the different landscapes into
this interior with the parrots of the jungle and the giant shell of the
ocean. Here they are married together to symbolise the fluidity of
the mountains to the sea in Ecuador.

I painted this wall one of my pinks – one coat gives it a textile
finish, a little uneven but all the better for it. Layer your interior
with the heady scent of garden roses. Flea-market finds, like this
small table and stool, are painted on a whim from our palette. The
scale of the shell sitting on almost an artist's stool makes it an
important piece – like a sculpture. It is a celebration of nature as
art. Interiors should not be very serious and the giant parrot candle
makes it fun! A simple addition that changes the mood.

Dr Garcia Moreno

[THESE PAGES] This is almost like a hotel room scenario. By this I mean that you have everything you need in a small space. Don't think you always have to do a formal furniture arrangement. This is particularly useful in a studio or boatshed space. I spend so much time in hotel rooms, beautiful ones, that there is something homely about having everything you need close by. You don't need to have a lot of space to be comfortable. Think of it as intimate, not small, and relish the advantages of not having a huge space to style, clean and inhabit. Be clever with editing and your stuff. For example, the collection of objets on the console works as a dividing mechanism in the room. It can be looked at and admired from both sides – change your objets for a fresh view. Smart furniture arrangement will create nooks to sit, read, write, work, converse in & have all the moments you would in a home of any size.

I visited a woman in her eighties, a family friend of one of my wayfaring companions. After downsizing from a mansion, she lived in an apartment, and collected lots of beautiful carved furniture, Olga Fisch rugs, religious icons, Viking-style leather and wood chairs, gold metal thread embroidered vests with alpaca, castle-style shields & other grandness. Amongst her many things were beautiful orchids of all kinds – definitely a collection in themselves. I'm sure this was a pint-size version of the former glory her home must have been – but it was enough and it fit just right.

[NEXT PAGES] Gus Angermeyer was one of the earliest settlers on Santa Cruz Island in the Galapagos. He left Germany in the 1930s and set out on an adventure with his brothers & a dream of a life at one with nature. There were only a few others already living on the island and the Angermeyers settled around the bay area to marry, raise their families & build boats for fishing. Their homes, many still standing today, were built from the natural resources available: lavastone, rocks & wood. You can stay here today, at the Angermeyer Waterfront Inn. The Cave was my favourite part – Gus used to read the works of Shakespeare and Einstein in this sanctuary of his and share his exciting adventures to those he invited in.

This space is like a kind of sanctuary or cool lookout. Create your own – even if it's not facing the sea. Lookouts & sanctuaries often inspire contemplation or offer a place to hide away. By making one in your home, you create a moment and space to breathe and reflect without climbing to the top of a lighthouse and staring into an expanse of ocean or escaping to your local cave.

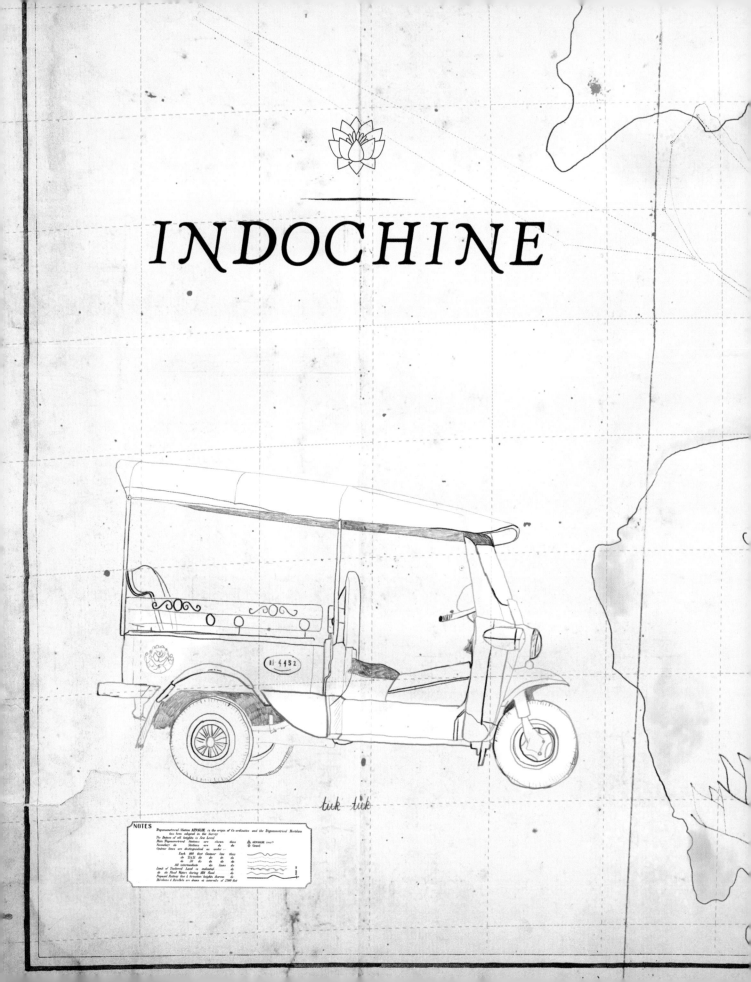

INDOCHINE

tuk tuk

flesh
pink

dilute

opa

sepia

Indochine

The area where Laos, Cambodia and Vietnam are on the map was once referred to as Indochine, or French Indochina. This was a time between 1884 and 1954 when the entire region was colonised by the French, and the name is a combination of China and India between which it sits. The term identified the borders of French rule and encompassed all the colonies within that had their own set boundaries.

I decided to name this chapter Indochine, not just because I visited these three countries, but because during these trips I saw things through the lens of a time past. When the region had the name Indochine, the romance of faraway lands and exotic lure of the Orient attracted travellers from all over the globe, and new modes of transport made adventures more possible.

Throughout Southeast Asia, shrines exist everywhere for both private & shared purposes. Offerings come in many shapes & forms: folded lotus flowers, coins & notes, cigarettes, flowers in garlands (marigolds, tuberose etc.), incense, folded & manipulated banana leaf, rice, fruit (banana, rambutan, lychee etc.) and alcohol.

One day, we visited the Golden City Temple (Wat Xieng Thong) in Laos, known for its elaborate story-telling mosaic mirrors in all different colours. I wandered away and discovered the working monastery behind the show. The scattering of buildings were whitewashed with peak-topped roofs and potted plants. There was a real honesty to it. With an abundance of shrines in all shapes and sizes, it was a very simple shrine I discovered here that encapsulated my colour palette. It appeared to be painted in a dulled gold with a buddha pride of place on a matte black base surrounded by a random scattering of offerings: sticky rice with its dirty white tone, a terracotta pot and a peony pink paintbrush.

Even though we were in the middle of the jungle and there were other colours everywhere, it didn't matter. The ochres were what the monks wore, the incense, and colour of a pink lotus petal or marigolds, paper decorations and the lovely clay colour of the Mekong. This set offered a perfect Indochine palette, which then made me see it in everything else.

I travelled on long wooden boats with central lounging areas and watched white-tipped butterflies skim along the surface of the Mekong River, passing secret water paths that led to hidden stilted houses and houseboats. The river was milky, the colour of clay and ochre. The weather was hot, but not raining, and my visions were heavy with tropical heat and warm colours. There is a quiet humbleness to Indochine that sits comfortably alongside the madness of tuktuks and motorbikes on the roads and bustling food markets with everything you could imagine stacked up & down and side to side.

lotus

patchouli

khmer

sticky rice

temple

monkey puzzle

lunar

lions & tigers

alms

Mekong

Throughout Indochine you see monks' robes in saffron and ochre, freshly washed and hanging up to dry wherever you go. Bring your textiles out and use them as screening devices or just to display. There is beauty in them floating within a space, rather than being up against a wall. My own throws & quilts are hanging from leather piano straps I found at auction, but use anything you have at hand.

[NEXT PAGES] A couple of hours down the Mekong from Luang Prabang, travelling by longboat, there is a cave that acts as a graveyard for broken or faded Buddhas. I love the journey you have to undertake for discoveries. At the top of all these steps, there was a collection of lovely, simple wooden chairs lined up like soldiers. Placed here for the much needed rest! I repeated the simplicity in the arrangement through my interior. We bought a cone-shaped banana leaf, encircled in marigolds, holding three saffron candles & incense sticks to offer & say a prayer.

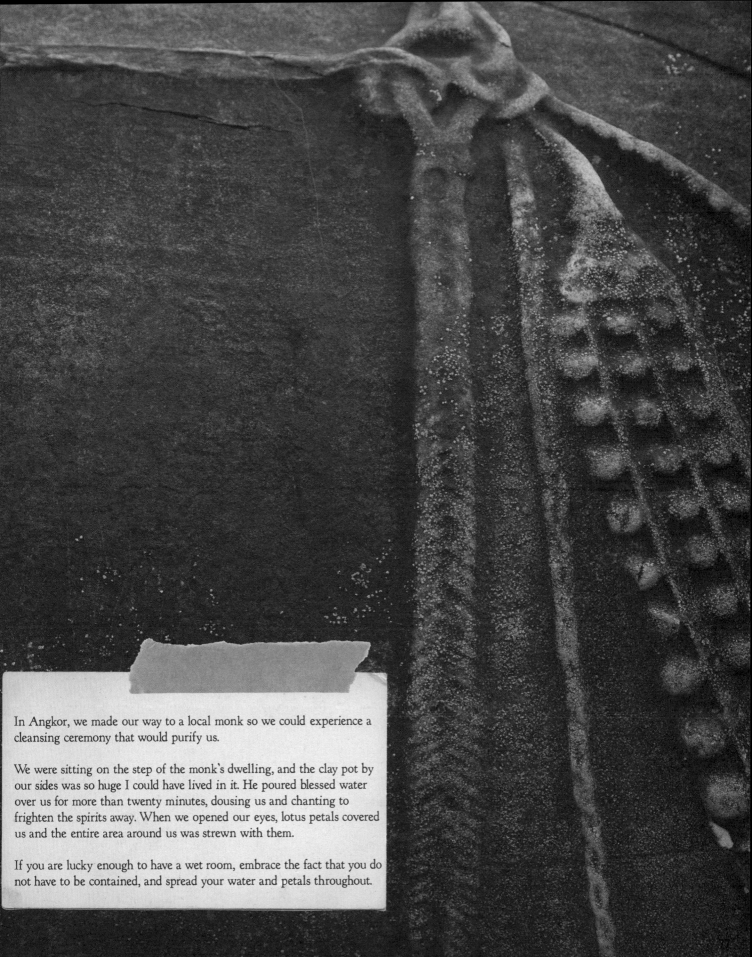

In Angkor, we made our way to a local monk so we could experience a cleansing ceremony that would purify us.

We were sitting on the step of the monk's dwelling, and the clay pot by our sides was so huge I could have lived in it. He poured blessed water over us for more than twenty minutes, dousing us and chanting to frighten the spirits away. When we opened our eyes, lotus petals covered us and the entire area around us was strewn with them.

If you are lucky enough to have a wet room, embrace the fact that you do not have to be contained, and spread your water and petals throughout.

Luang Prabang is on a peninsula and we rode our
bikes everywhere! After visiting monks at
5 am, we stopped for a breakfast of coffee,
croissants & lemon soda at a café, Le Banneton, in
a lovely restored colonial house.

The morning of my first day in Angkor Wat,
running through the rain on huge flagstones to the
shelter of a tree where a utilitarian wood table and
benches sat, shiny & wet from the downpour.

Plain spaces have their beauty, and both these
experiences inspired this simple set. Sometimes you
need no more.

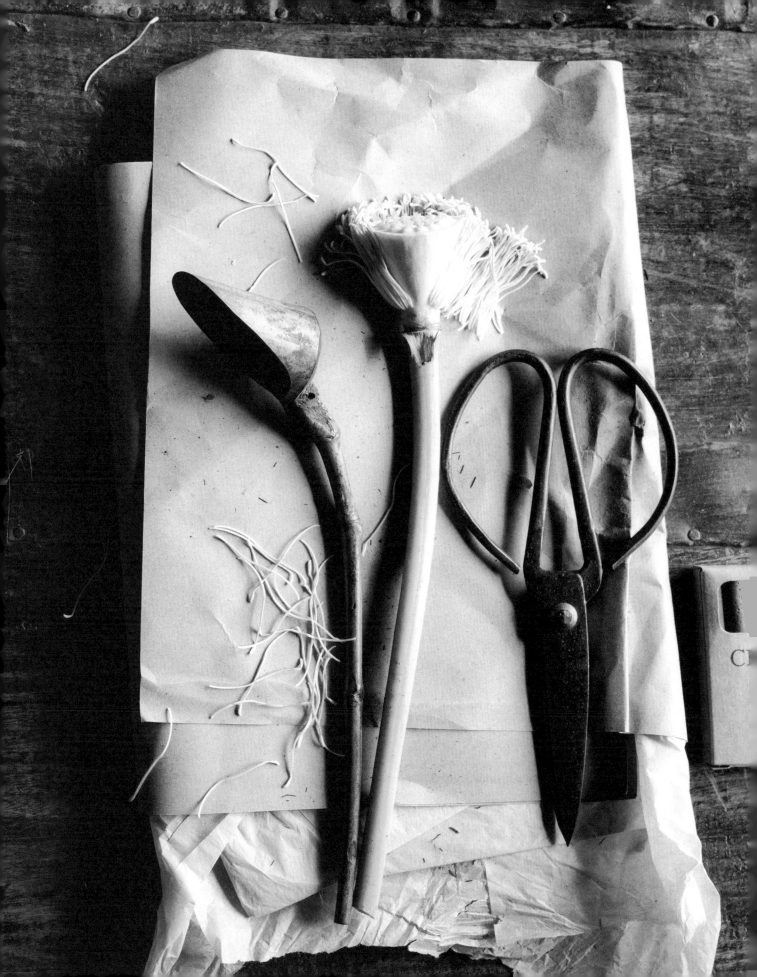

[PREVIOUS PAGES] A favourite travelling pastime is
to visit the everyday food markets and see what other
cultures eat & grow and how they store, package and
transport their goods. Use your memories to create a
tabletop still-life and see how a real-life memory can be
interpreted in a small way.

Take note of the remnants of things. Andrea Gentl (a
fabulous NYC photographer) was always making me
look at the beauty in what was left behind. You can see
this a lot in the travel pics.

[THESE PAGES] On an amazing tuktuk, wooden
panelled with balustrades, cream fabric upholstered seats,
wicker picnic baskets attached to the back, and black
umbrellas just in case, we headed into the jungle. It got
so dense that we jumped on motorcycles to plunge up
& over an invisible path leading us to a giant sleeping
Buddha carved out of the stone mountain. A catwalk-
style temple was built around it, narrow and clinging to
the rock. We walked around it three times in offering
and to make our hopes come true. On the ground in
front of the absolute beauty of the Buddha were the most
unexpected, worn geometric tiles. The pattern stayed
with me and I have translated this through this rug. As
well, the element of repetition speaks to me through the
pattern I chalked on the wall and the feeling of serenity
I wanted this office space to have. Look for repeat
patterns in your travels to interpret once home in a more
simple way.

[THESE PAGES] At 5 am, the monks of many temples hit the streets with singing bowls in hand. The streets are lined with plastic geometric mats and bamboo-lidded woven vessels containing sticky rice for alms. My own version of the plastic mats for lounging on low-seated furniture, and wooden beaded lights stacked like sculptural stone towers found through the ancient temples of Angkor Wat.

[NEXT PAGES] On a super early morning we escaped out the back door of the resort to watch the sun rise and wander around the lakes. The waterlilies were welcoming the day and their pop of colour against a neutral background was heavenly. The imagery speaks in this bedroom. The bed is made with linens drawn from around the globe.

Staying at the Amansara, an enclosed
stone & garden compound built in
1962 for King Norodom Sihanouk as a
guesthouse, was very James Bond-esque.
The King wanted Cambodia to be cool.
The modern circular building housing
the dining room & front pool of the
hotel (or other home as it is often called)
was his screening room as hot-looking
people lazed around the swimming pool.
These Erik Buch chairs are the essence of
modern – recognisable and classic – but
here they sit by a lopsided brass vase and
frangipanis to add the exotic element of
the Orient. The burst of yellow allows the
stools to sit comfortably in this setting. I
love how a colour palette can join together
a mixture of textures, shapes and pieces
from different design eras.

LANTERN &
2 CELL 3606.

CUPBOARD
NO 9

107

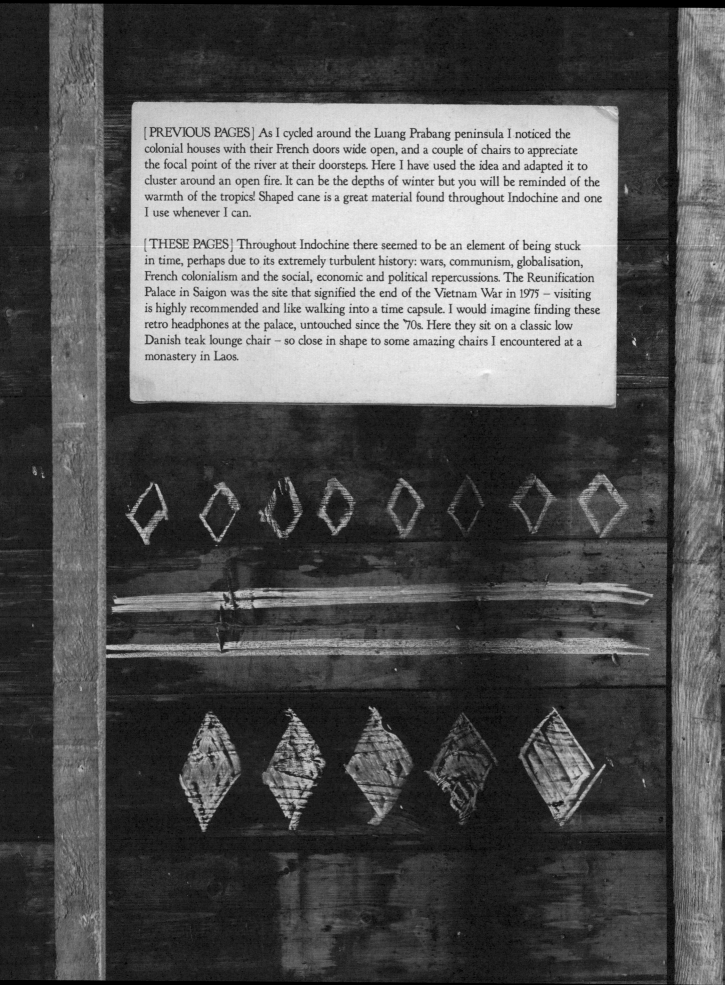

[PREVIOUS PAGES] As I cycled around the Luang Prabang peninsula I noticed the colonial houses with their French doors wide open, and a couple of chairs to appreciate the focal point of the river at their doorsteps. Here I have used the idea and adapted it to cluster around an open fire. It can be the depths of winter but you will be reminded of the warmth of the tropics! Shaped cane is a great material found throughout Indochine and one I use whenever I can.

[THESE PAGES] Throughout Indochine there seemed to be an element of being stuck in time, perhaps due to its extremely turbulent history: wars, communism, globalisation, French colonialism and the social, economic and political repercussions. The Reunification Palace in Saigon was the site that signified the end of the Vietnam War in 1975 – visiting is highly recommended and like walking into a time capsule. I would imagine finding these retro headphones at the palace, untouched since the '70s. Here they sit on a classic low Danish teak lounge chair – so close in shape to some amazing chairs I encountered at a monastery in Laos.

In Luang Prabang and Saigon, the daily food markets are a treat. Much of the foodstuffs are packaged with bamboo and woven basketry. Live chickens & ducks jostle for room in open-weave stacked baskets, crabs are tied with bamboo to reduce the risk of nips and for easy carrying, almost like a handbag. Use these everyday materials in a decorative way, here they are lanterns but you could even electrify them to use as pendants.

[THESE PAGES] Look sky
high on your travels, you never
know what you may discover.
It might be a hot-air balloon
or beautiful paper fancies and
flags surrounding temples.
A variation on this theme is
found in this handmade, naïve
chandelier. Never forget to
utilise the up-space and play
with scale. This has become a
corner of magic and fancy to
read or study in.

[NEXT PAGES] A random
assortment of things to inspire
reflection, this one still-life
speaks of many calm and
personal moments throughout
my travels.

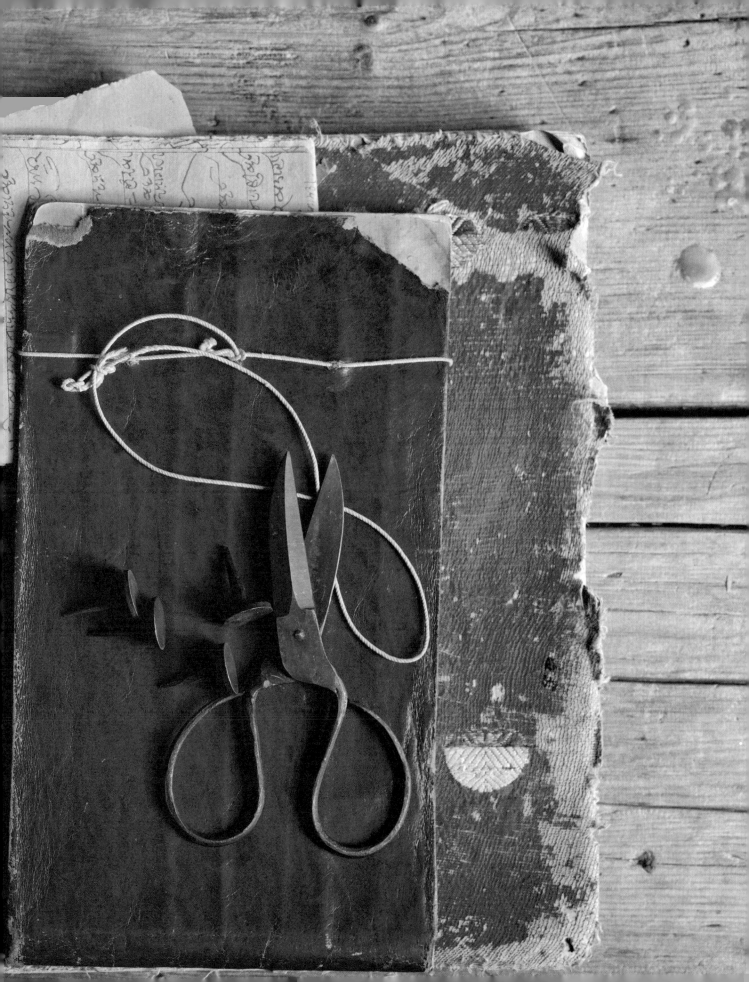

In many of the temples, shrines and monasteries there were columns, both interior and exterior, painted in chalky matte black.

Sometimes it was quite patchy and old; other times you could see it had been recently refreshed. It was layered with a gold paint stencil. Use this pattern to inspire your bed linen.

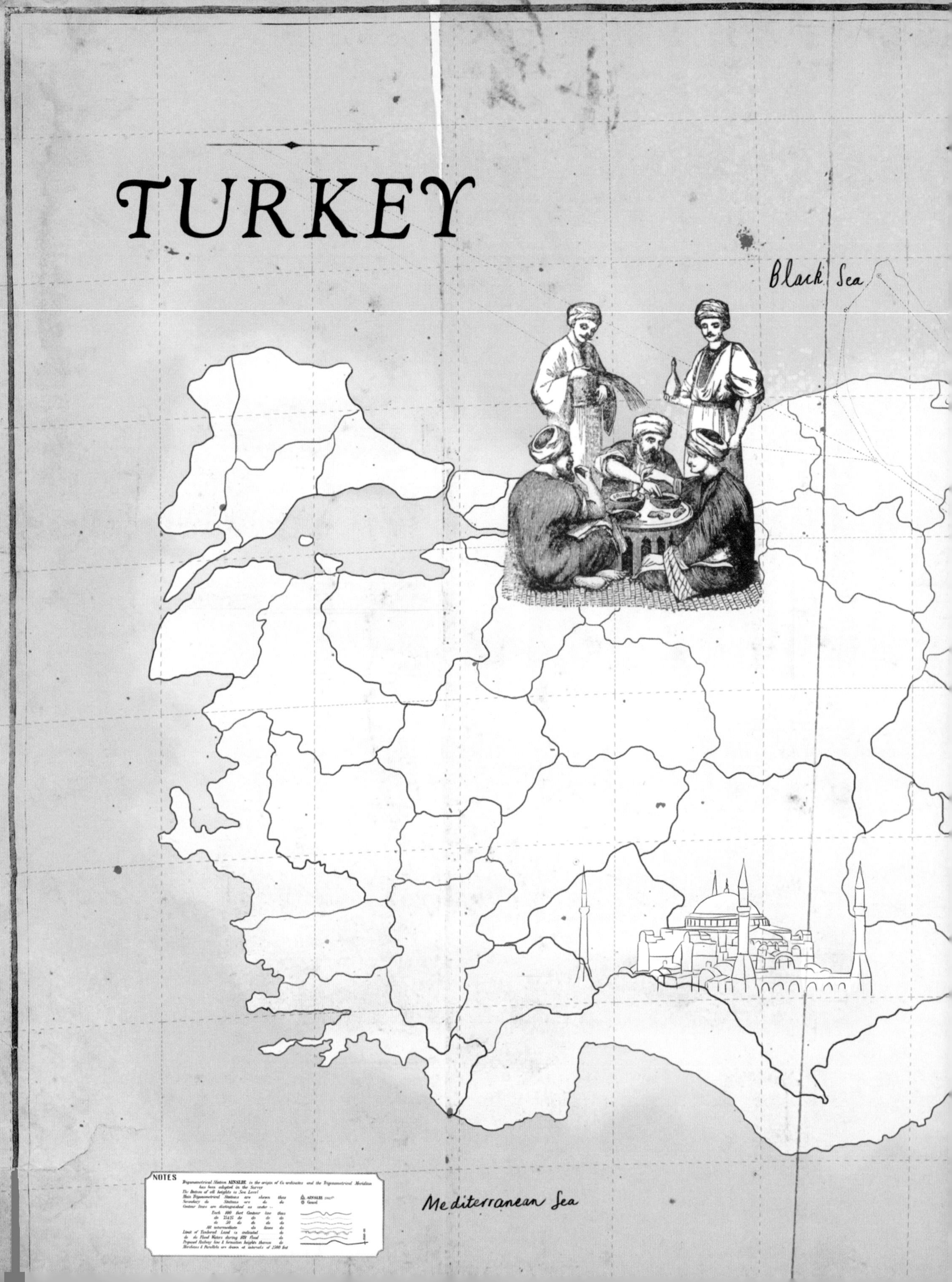
TURKEY
Black Sea
Mediterranean Sea
NOTES

Turkey

For many, Turkey conjures up pictures of the Grand Bazaar and the hustle & bustle of Istanbul. Without intention, I found a quiet amongst this and my inspiration came from the gulets, waterways and meeting of the seas as well as textiles, architecture and Iznik tiles. You find your own way in all places that you visit, and sometimes it is the path less trodden. Istanbul has been a port since ancient times because of its geographical positioning. I imagine ships of all sizes in the harbour carrying textiles & treasures from countries that surround Turkey & beyond, seamen rubbing shoulders with fortune-tellers & seers, traders & dervishes! My mother had visited Turkey many times as a textile lover & collector, and I thought of her as I travelled and discovered traders & their wares as she would have. Her collections, much like my own, are a reflection of her travels, love, aesthetic & knowledge.

In Bodrum I sailed on the Aegean Sea where the water was crystal clear, turquoise, very salty, floaty, silvery and full of sea gypsies. There was an absolute clarity in the colours. Sails unravelled in all their glory as they were hoisted to full mast to reflect the sun.

Travelling along the coast, towns were full of seaside activity: red & blue fishing nets piled high, villagers working on boats, and seafood restaurants where you can taste the catch of the day. In Gümüsluk, a small shop selling home-made marmalade brought warm tones into a cool backdrop. But ultimately, Turkey's colours came in a moment, and then spoke to me over the rest of the trip. A shoe shiner with his tools, sandals and shoe-shining equipment presented a collection of blues, oranges and red. Perhaps if I had started my trip in the rabbit warren that is the Grand Bazaar, my palette would be based around the rich colours & textures of the goods within, but this trip was founded in a very different experience.

I travelled across the lands, north to Istanbul, where I stayed at Hotel Empress Zoe. My mum stayed here many moons ago & it was a favourite haunt of hers. Higgledy-piggledy with 26 rooms and up & down marble stairs surrounding the leafy, wisteria-covered internal garden full of secret spots to discover. All of this made me consider missing some sightseeing to enjoy the serenity.

My room was a small apartment with two large rooms, suzanis galore and hand-carved marble washbasins similar to those you see in hammams. Arched doorways led from one room to the next with softly sheered windows on one side and a small balcony overlooking the garden on the other. Lots of space to think and relax.

I spent my time in the city looking skyward at the Blue Mosque and Hagia Sophia, stumbling upon the incredible patterns of Iznik tiles, Turkish architecture that speaks across the centuries, the Archaeological Museum, and textiles in bazaars. Even here there was a stillness, a tribute to the sea and moments to spend drinking thick muddy Turkish coffee and reflecting on the goings-on.

marmara

treasureseeker

knight 1492

ahoy

bitter orange

dervish

iznik

ancient mariner

crusader

To get into the mood in Turkey, the Anthropologie crew and I set sail on the Aegean Sea. We head north, up the coast (this may not be nautically correct) past islands so small you can't even find them on Google. I named these mystery islands the Orkas, because there was nothing to stop me. We swim in 20-degree water, admiring its translucency, and get into the swing of things with mezze and rosé.

I loosely wrapped old ferry rope around a column and hung a pond sailor found in a junk store on the wall. Splattered water cushion and the dip-dyed knitted piece used as window treatment are reminiscent of fishing nets and sea tones.

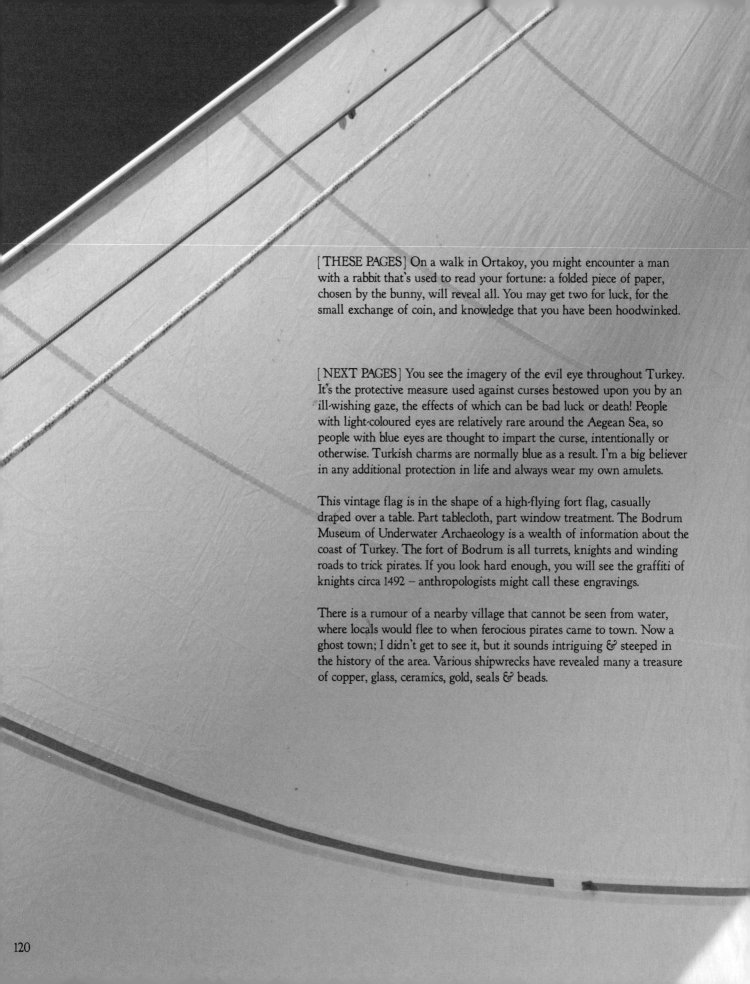

[THESE PAGES] On a walk in Ortakoy, you might encounter a man with a rabbit that's used to read your fortune: a folded piece of paper, chosen by the bunny, will reveal all. You may get two for luck, for the small exchange of coin, and knowledge that you have been hoodwinked.

[NEXT PAGES] You see the imagery of the evil eye throughout Turkey. It's the protective measure used against curses bestowed upon you by an ill-wishing gaze, the effects of which can be bad luck or death! People with light-coloured eyes are relatively rare around the Aegean Sea, so people with blue eyes are thought to impart the curse, intentionally or otherwise. Turkish charms are normally blue as a result. I'm a big believer in any additional protection in life and always wear my own amulets.

This vintage flag is in the shape of a high-flying fort flag, casually draped over a table. Part tablecloth, part window treatment. The Bodrum Museum of Underwater Archaeology is a wealth of information about the coast of Turkey. The fort of Bodrum is all turrets, knights and winding roads to trick pirates. If you look hard enough, you will see the graffiti of knights circa 1492 – anthropologists might call these engravings.

There is a rumour of a nearby village that cannot be seen from water, where locals would flee to when ferocious pirates came to town. Now a ghost town; I didn't get to see it, but it sounds intriguing & steeped in the history of the area. Various shipwrecks have revealed many a treasure of copper, glass, ceramics, gold, seals & beads.

Swing from chandeliers

Bodies of water
lapping at the
shores of Turkey

Bosphorus
The Golden Horn
Sea of Marmara
Black Sea
Mediterranean
Dardanelles
Aegian

[PREVIOUS PAGES] This room has the proportions of Hagia Sophia or another large mosque. I've emulated their domes with the beautiful fabric pendant lamp.

Choosing this dotted coverlet is a loose interpretation of springtime in Turkey. All the parks are in full bloom – tulips for days! The reds jumped for me and if I were to sleep in this bed, I would dream of sleeping under poppies.

The geometric patterns of the rug can be seen throughout Istanbul in amazing Iznik tilework. Because of its location, the city has been a port since ancient times. It's where East meets West and the coming together of three bodies of water – the Sea of Marmara, the Golden Horn and the Bosphorus. This significance is translated through the gradation of blue in the Ercol chair, an obvious reference to water.

[THESE PAGES] When Istanbul was Constantinople, the capital of the Byzantine Empire, Constantine the Great defended the city at all costs. Defensive stone walls were built on land and in the water. Enemy access to Istanbul's deep natural harbour, the Golden Horn, was thwarted by a heavy chain across the mouth of the inlet.

I was always looking forward to sitting in the garden at my hotel & whiling away the afternoon after adventures through the city in the morning. As I lounge and relax, I hear birds galore, the action of the busy port with boat horns, the happy chatter of visitors, and dice on wooden backgammon boards. Rooftops are utilised here with dining & gardens to make the most of the weather & domed skyline. Views are of the busy waterways of the Bosphorus and Sea of Marmara, the call to prayer plays as the soundtrack and, as evening settles, a sliver moon hovers above in clear skies.

The bed with dip-dyed mosquito nets the colour of the Bosphorus and rope chains, which wouldn't deter many, take you back to another time.

Make your own woven tablecloth with paper tape.
The famous Iznik tiles of Turkey surround you in
the architecture of mosques and when you're out &
about, and their patterns are mind-blowing. This is
my own, somewhat naïve version.

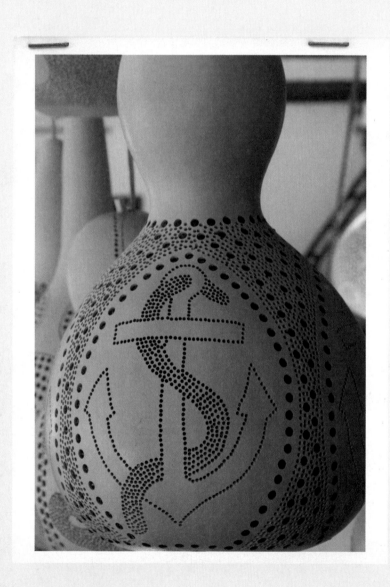

I'm into interference at the moment. *Gypsy* is about going back to your own things, and interfering with them. Add a new colour palette – this one is Turkey, but through objet choice it could have sat happily in any other one of the chapters. Here I took a few things down and added other pieces from around & about in the colour palette to totally change the feel. In the background, the band Mt Warning were jamming as we shot on a glorious March day. Not a travel soundscape, but a new memory all the same.

The mountains fall into the sea on the coastal drive to Gumusluk. Along a short, windy road, tiny blood-red spring poppies grow, and the shadows from the mountains forever in the background make the Aegean Sea look like a lake. Villagers sell gourds on the roadside, painted white with many holes to let the light shine through. The local artisan market we discovered when we arrived was well worth the visit. Wonderful small stalls filled with ceramics I couldn't resist and surrounded by orchards of olive & citrus groves. Shopping is rewarded with lunch overlooking the sea.

If you want to revisit a travel memory, pick appropriate tableware and textiles and channel your destination over lunch.

After an informative morning at Bodrum Castle, which houses the Museum of Underwater Archaeology, we had lunch with diver/physicist/ guide Don Frey. He led us to the best mezze in town which, of course, finished with thick, muddy Turkish coffee, served in outfits of decorative silver armour, peak hatted & all. On draining our coffees, Don instructed us to think of a question/desire, rotate the cup three times, turn it onto the saucer & leave it for a while to let the grinds cascade down. Then the cup was flipped & you could read the grinds on the ceramic interior. To me, it looked like mountains, peaks & precipices – a time of reflection & a slower pace.

AHOY: To be shouted with a cupped hand announcing your arrival to shore (or anywhere really). Use your colour palette and add 3D detail with string art, easy to do yourself at home with a little help from the internet or a talented friend.

The most amazing range of textiles is on show in Istanbul, a selection from Turkey's eight bordering countries and beyond. A mess of colours & textures in pieced rugs, kilim, sheepskin, rag rugs, ikat from Anatolia, velvet & silk by the yard, suzanis, camel blankets, hammam towels, old & new, Moroccan-style Turkish rugs and very plain white & blue colour palettes from Iran.

Old broken pond sailor found at
a junk store and rigged up with
rope. No screws needed.

Although I found this in Porte de Vanves flea market in Paris, it is a universal reference to the perfect seaside still-life. In this setting, it reminds me of the coast of Turkey.

This is a long, lazy afternoon drinking lots of muddy, Turkish coffee and playing backgammon over & over with the soundscape of dice on a wooden board. Here I have brought it together with bunting that's strung through Turkish boats. This memory is based on my first trip to Turkey with a past love. I imagine I would be playing with the captain as we came into port or perhaps in the Egyptian spice bazaar which makes for hours of exploring, and negotiating with strange traders over mint tea with sugar, apricots, almonds & pistachios, nougat and Turkish delight. I can just imagine the atmosphere that must have existed here as people from along the Silk Route exchanged stories and bargains.

The rug is a hexagonal shape, but I call it tortoiseshell. You see this repeat pattern on lots of floors and walls throughout the country, from stone to tiles, to all sorts of things.

[THESE PAGES] I love a low-lying bed. Every seaman has a sea chest that holds all of his worldly possessions & treasures. Often highly decorated, I've gone with something a little more simple and used it as my headboard. No need to match your sheets, use a white as your base and layer with your colour palette.

I went to Cagaloglu Hammam, avoided the loofah scrub (bit rough for my skin) but went for a lie-around on the marble slab. I found a little hidden room through a small doorway, all marble & arches & vistas & steamy, the sound of water everywhere, and the light soft as it filters through the carved skylights in the dome.

Note: there is a shop in most hammams and it's a good idea to purchase (or bring) some olive oil soap, a little kinder on the skin than the supplied one.

There is such romance in these carved, smooth, marbled women-only bathhouses. Often they have the central circular hot stone to lie & have a massage on, then alcoves & exterior smaller rooms with a marble washbasin with beautiful brass taps. Once you have purchased your service, scrub, massage etc., you can stay as long as you like. Always rejuvenating & refreshing.

The long lunch in Bodrum with Don Frey was made up of lots of different mezze plates and went on for hours. Invoke that atmosphere of afternoon casualness and a sense of sharing with plates of different sizes and whatever glasses you happen to have. Even if you're not outside, it will feel like it.

151

SCOTLAND

Harris

North Atlantic Sea

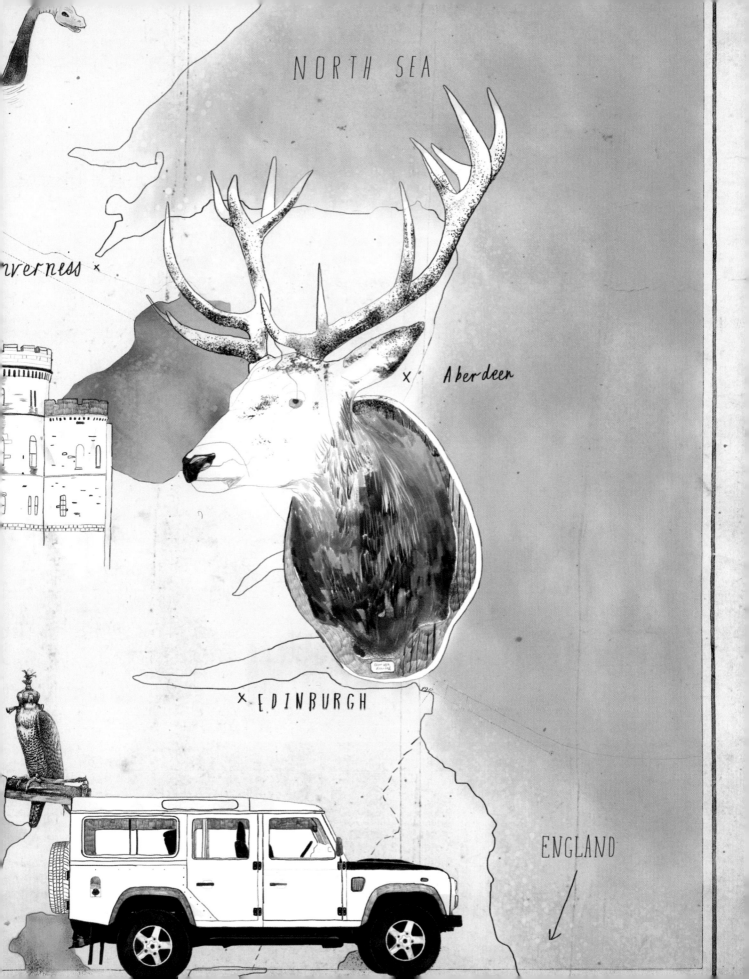

NORTH SEA

nverness ×

× Aberdeen

× EDINBURGH

ENGLAND

tail feather

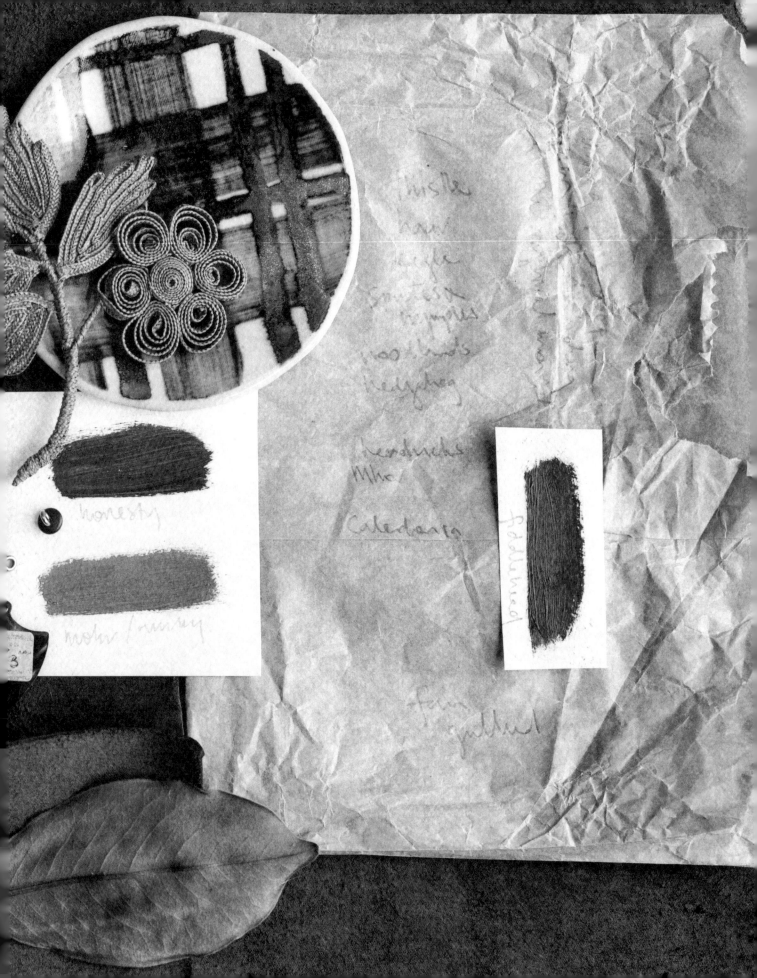

Thistle
bed
eagle
Souesa
trumpets
rose buds
Hedgehog

burdocks
Mho

Caledonia

honesty

mohr/rusty

fiddlehead

fern
fiddlehead

Scotland

My father's birthday & an excuse to finally get to Scotland led us on our road trip. He's a fabulous companion as he is up for any adventure & considers himself a road warrior. His thoughts of Scotland ran to checking out caramel shaggy longhorns, trying out some single malts, island hopping in a cream Defender, and putting on a Scottish accent with little success. I had visions of Charles Darwin foraging at the Firth of Forth, falconry & archery, castles, moors & the Highlands, taxidermy, trophy heads & tartan.

We caught the train from London to Edinburgh, and travelling up the east coast of Scotland saw the haar roll in. This coastal fog comes in off the North Sea and smothers everything in its wake. Grey had to be one of the colours in the Scottish palette, although for most of the rest of our trip, the weather couldn't have been better. The soft grey was there, too, in the weathered stone of Edinburgh's buildings, slated roofs and cobblestone streets, in lochs and in the Loch Ness monster, although he was too shy to reveal himself to me.

A much-anticipated falconry lesson offered all deep browns and soft caramels in feathers, claw-proof suede gauntlets and leather hoods. Those same tones were also found in comical shaggy Highland cattle on a backdrop of impossibly green fields and again in whisky, which we sipped with a water chaser in old-fashioned inns.

As we traversed the Highlands and isles of Scotland, a very obvious palette revealed itself in the expected and the unexpected.

The tiny bell-shaped heather flower carpets every hillside of the Highlands landscape giving it an overall smoky soft purple tone with a scent that smells of the earth. It's so springy to walk on, and is tough enough to make brooms and brushes from – and is also very lucky in a gypsy kind of way. At Jupiter Artland we walk into Anya Gallaccio's magical amethyst sunken grotto and are surrounded by a deep chamber of amethyst encrusted walls – so magical in the range of purple hues that complement the landscape outside.

The Gulf Stream swings right past the west coast of Scotland, meaning that Inverewe Garden is full of palms and other unexpected tropical plants. Created in 1862 and sheltered by 40 hectares of woodlands, this is an oasis of bright greens amongst the Highlands. When Dad and I were driving north on hedge-lined lanes, we passed a few lovely old-fashioned sports cars in British racing green with go-fast stripes, the kind of cars that leather goggles need to be worn to drive.

Our last night in Scotland was at Bramble Bield, in a gypsy caravan for Dad & a 1920s travelling caravan for me, in gardens with glasshouses full of luscious young seedlings & vegetable patches, all very Peter Rabbit-y & story tale-ish.

honesty

barnacle

hedgehog

longhorn

1513

tailfeather

Caledonian

fiddlehead

thistle

haar

Rhuveag

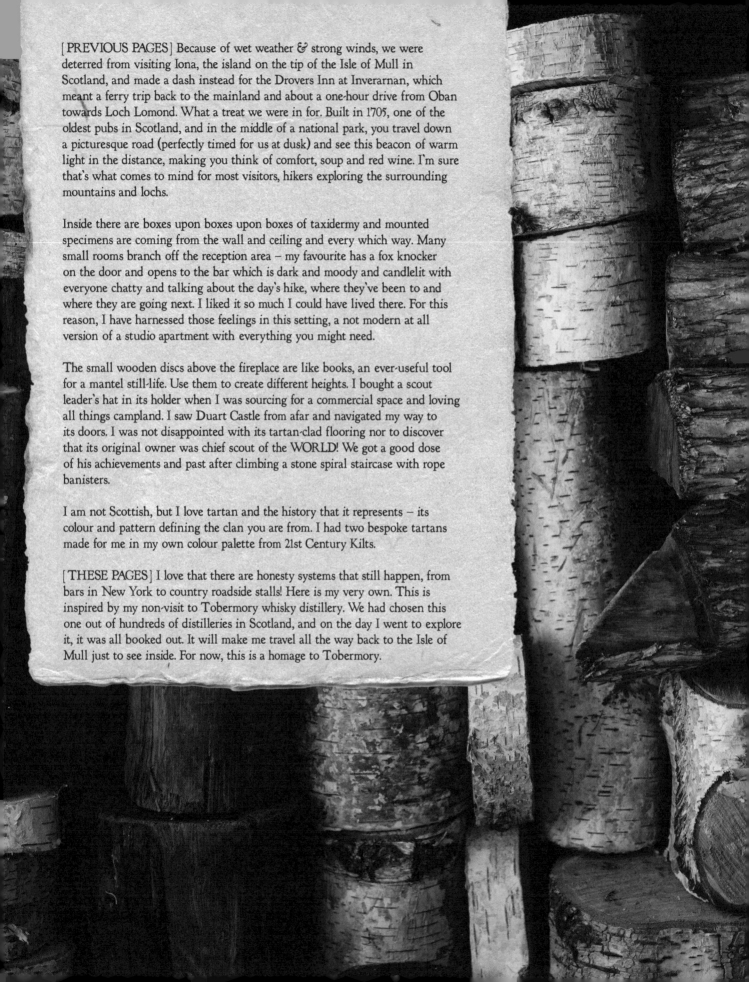

[PREVIOUS PAGES] Because of wet weather & strong winds, we were deterred from visiting Iona, the island on the tip of the Isle of Mull in Scotland, and made a dash instead for the Drovers Inn at Inverarnan, which meant a ferry trip back to the mainland and about a one-hour drive from Oban towards Loch Lomond. What a treat we were in for. Built in 1705, one of the oldest pubs in Scotland, and in the middle of a national park, you travel down a picturesque road (perfectly timed for us at dusk) and see this beacon of warm light in the distance, making you think of comfort, soup and red wine. I'm sure that's what comes to mind for most visitors, hikers exploring the surrounding mountains and lochs.

Inside there are boxes upon boxes upon boxes of taxidermy and mounted specimens are coming from the wall and ceiling and every which way. Many small rooms branch off the reception area – my favourite has a fox knocker on the door and opens to the bar which is dark and moody and candlelit with everyone chatty and talking about the day's hike, where they've been to and where they are going next. I liked it so much I could have lived there. For this reason, I have harnessed those feelings in this setting, a not modern at all version of a studio apartment with everything you might need.

The small wooden discs above the fireplace are like books, an ever-useful tool for a mantel still-life. Use them to create different heights. I bought a scout leader's hat in its holder when I was sourcing for a commercial space and loving all things campland. I saw Duart Castle from afar and navigated my way to its doors. I was not disappointed with its tartan-clad flooring nor to discover that its original owner was chief scout of the WORLD! We got a good dose of his achievements and past after climbing a stone spiral staircase with rope banisters.

I am not Scottish, but I love tartan and the history that it represents – its colour and pattern defining the clan you are from. I had two bespoke tartans made for me in my own colour palette from 21st Century Kilts.

[THESE PAGES] I love that there are honesty systems that still happen, from bars in New York to country roadside stalls! Here is my very own. This is inspired by my non-visit to Tobermory whisky distillery. We had chosen this one out of hundreds of distilleries in Scotland, and on the day I went to explore it, it was all booked out. It will make me travel all the way back to the Isle of Mull just to see inside. For now, this is a homage to Tobermory.

Essentials for a road trip: map, fruit knife, oat biscuits, aged cheddar, good music, Dad. Always look out for a knife while you're travelling, it's a great little souvenir and super handy on the road (just make sure not to leave it in your carry-on luggage on the way home).

SOLINGEN-GERMANY
STAINLESS STEEL

This has elements from one of my favourite childhood books,
The Magic Faraway Tree – in fact, it is what I picture it to
look like at the very top! I went for a walk with my dad and we
discovered wooden steps that climbed all the way up the highest
pine I had ever seen. Up & up until they disappeared from view.
If I had ascended, I know I would have found Dame Washalot
and Moonface and everyone else.

[THESE PAGES] Roads in Scotland are lochside, one lane and super thin with a tiny overtaking bay every now and again. You can go for a long time without seeing anyone, save a sailing boat on the loch you're passing by. Even if the vegetation of where you live isn't like Scotland, you can re-create the overwhelming feeling of green and lushness by creating your own magical forest. If you don't have access to these string balls, just cut foliage and put it in vases at all different heights. This achieves a feeling of being surrounded, and mimics mountains and lakes which are never at an even keel.

[NEXT PAGES] My homage to the night I spent with my dad at Bramble Bield.

A cluster of two old wooden gypsy caravans and a 1920s travelling car, all restored with love, are parked in the grounds of Powis House alongside picturesque fields of woolly sheep. I had opted for the dark green gypsy caravan 'Holly' painted with a prancing horse for Dad, and 'Bramley' the traditional travelling caravan for myself.

Holly comes with its own mini pot-belly stove that's fed with tiny kindling & miniature quarter logs, a large floating bed covered with a handmade quilt & fairy lights to boot. A hand-painted zigzag-topped pot houses some lovely old wooden gypsy pegs.

Bramley is simplicity at its best: a cream painted interior furnished with bunk beds made in the old campbed style of canvas, eyelets & rope, a spindle back chair, green wooden chest of drawers and sheepskin on wooden floorboards. A piece of dried fungus & a tiny hand-painted tile of a long-horned cow adorn the walls. The gardens of the house are worth a wander with glasshouses, a vegetable patch, high-rise rabbit warrens (yes, they live in the trunk of a tree), a weeping elm & moss-covered sheds to explore & discover.

Manners were very important in our household when I was growing up and I think there's a lot to be said for table etiquette. You can take the formality, and then loosen it up. I took a very formal table setting and relaxed it by adding a leather machinery belt and strewn flowers.

The Gulf Stream is a powerful, warm and swift ocean current that starts at the tip of Florida and makes its way across the Atlantic Ocean to northern Scotland. It creates an unexpectedly warm climate in what is otherwise known for wet, rug-up kind of weather. The Highlands are typically mossy, scrubby and lush but at Inverewe Garden you discover plants that normally sit on a tropical island or in the desert! It was all so unexpected – to invoke this, make a decorative arrangement out of something unusual like prickly pear.

Rabbits Jackdaw

Scottish

Red Squirrel

Pine Marten

Harvest Mouse

Poll Cat

Weasel

Stoat

Ferret

Orkney Vole

189

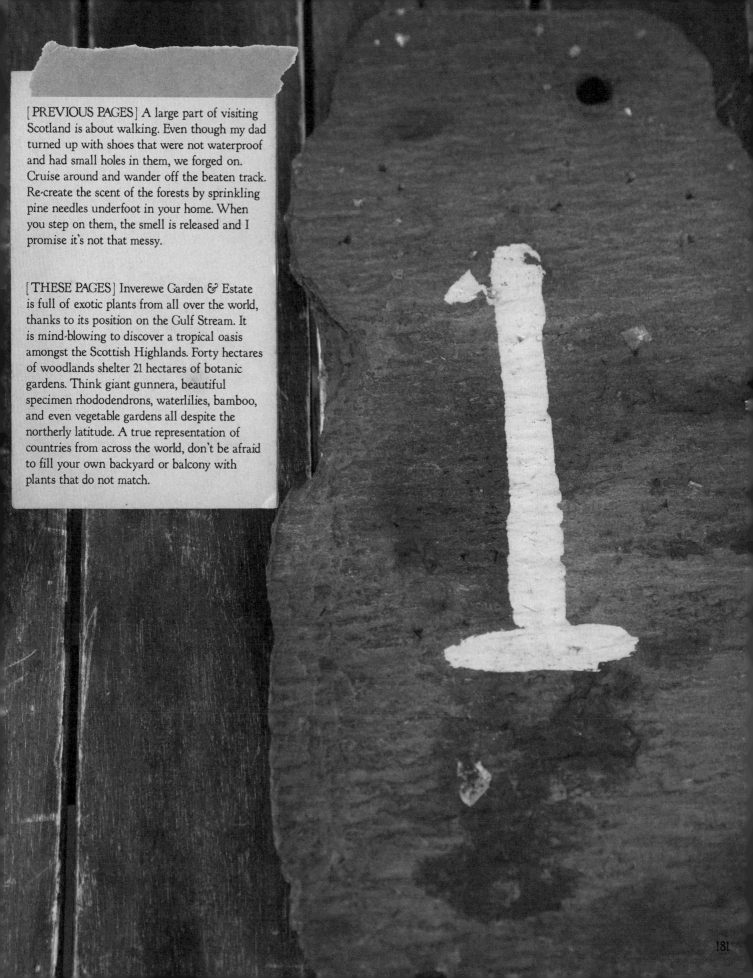

[PREVIOUS PAGES] A large part of visiting Scotland is about walking. Even though my dad turned up with shoes that were not waterproof and had small holes in them, we forged on. Cruise around and wander off the beaten track. Re-create the scent of the forests by sprinkling pine needles underfoot in your home. When you step on them, the smell is released and I promise it's not that messy.

[THESE PAGES] Inverewe Garden & Estate is full of exotic plants from all over the world, thanks to its position on the Gulf Stream. It is mind-blowing to discover a tropical oasis amongst the Scottish Highlands. Forty hectares of woodlands shelter 21 hectares of botanic gardens. Think giant gunnera, beautiful specimen rhododendrons, waterlilies, bamboo, and even vegetable gardens all despite the northerly latitude. A true representation of countries from across the world, don't be afraid to fill your own backyard or balcony with plants that do not match.

[PREVIOUS PAGES] I have always been attracted to humble materials. Those that have a utilitarian purpose, such as a flour sack, are now used as upholstery on a sofa and as a window treatment. A defunct fireplace can add an extra layer onto a wall; stack it tightly with birch rounds or wood from other trees you love. Flat things are good souvenirs – I often buy paintings that can slip between my clothes in my suitcase for a safe return. This oil painting is from Unicorn Antiques in Edinburgh.

[THESE PAGES] One of my main reasons for visiting Scotland was to follow the footsteps of a young Darwin, once a student of Edinburgh University, who used to scour the shores collecting barnacles & other specimens. Do your own foraging & fossicking, locally or while you're globetrotting, and display in a personal cabinet of curiosities. You may not write the next *Origin of Species*, but it creates a lovely quiet moment in your home to admire as you pass by.

SHALLOTS

188

[PREVIOUS PAGES] I love to mix old and new – here I was inspired by Strongarbh House on the Isle of Mull, a car ferry ride away from Oban on the west coast of Scotland. We discovered it through an Instagram recommendation. The lovingly restored house on the hill has had many reincarnations throughout its life from a morgue to an officer's mess and home. Enter to a flagstoned hallway and big wooden staircase, and two front rooms that look over Tobermory port. The library is all whitewashed light & modern (I think Ilse Crawford had some influence here) with beautiful, deep, shuttered windows. There are painted grey floorboards (more people should do this) in the gallery with a B&B Italia sectional sofa/ottoman and *Monocle* magazines. You can have a beautiful old building but it does not mean that everything you own has to be old! I might be attracted to pieces from the past time and time again, but I love modern. It was done to perfection at Strongarbh, by resting on their traditional foundations but creating a modern space.

[THESE PAGES] A timberyard to begin with, then an old prop house and theatre, now it is a restaurant & an Edinburgh must-go, and a source of inspiration here. Simply propped, you walk into Timberyard toward a ramp and there's an old leather-topped gymnasium vault and candles. A central courtyard is the perfect place to admire the space and enjoy your Hendricks served with cucumber, and tartan rugs to keep you warm.

Timberyard is tactile, subtle & perfectly executed and the family who run it are absolutely lovely. Don't disregard the importance of simplicity in styling, use this as a reference point and be excited about uncomplicated wall art and the quiet moment it can achieve. Here, single antlers shed by their original owners are strung up.

[NEXT PAGES] The littlest things can remind you of a place. I just added some loch-y ferns to my new, old kitchen made by master blacksmith Saul. As I am part-gypsy, there is no need for stoves & ovens in my kitchen. I work with a cast iron burner and it caters for all my needs. Don't feel like your rooms have to have all the mod cons – install only what you'll use and suits your lifestyle.

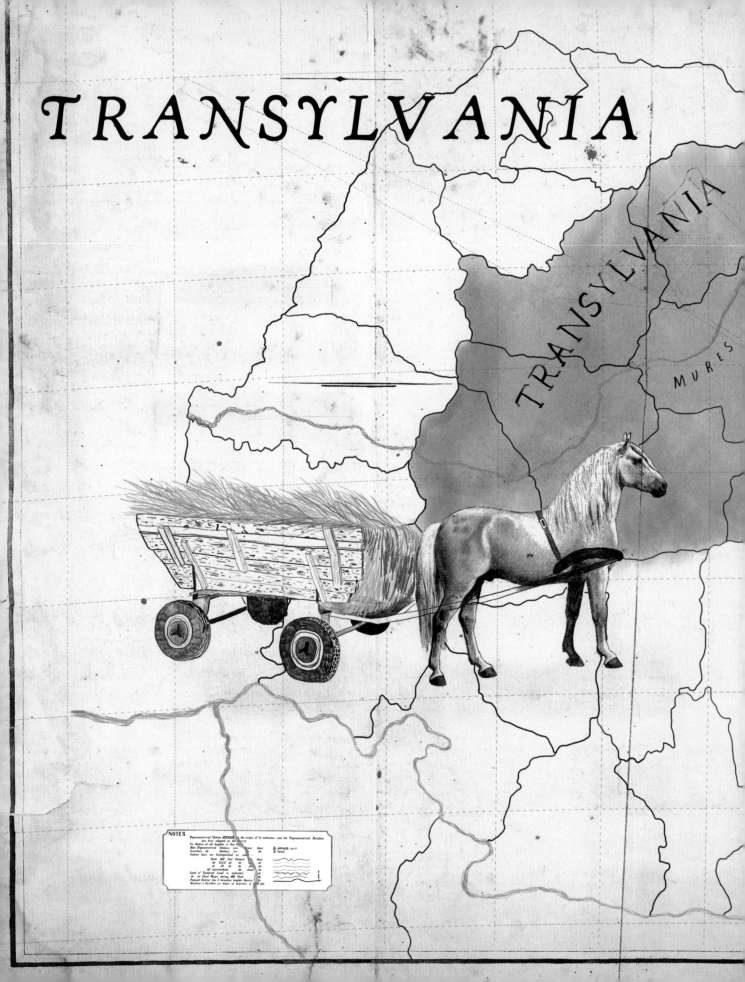

DANUBE

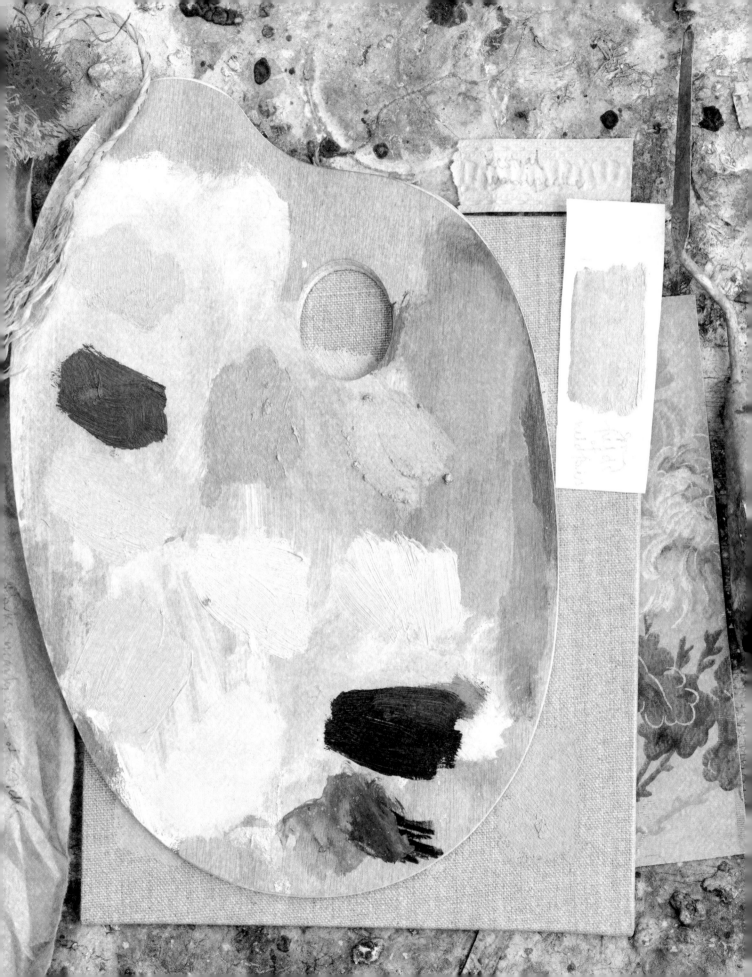

Transylvania

My romantic vision of Transylvania is filled with gypsies in colourfully painted caravans, layered skirts, horse whispering and music. I visited at the beginning of spring with my great friend James Merrell, when it was as if the whole world was about to bloom. The days were warm and cloudless, crisp in the morning and fresh. The landscape was a vision of soft, muted colours. I can only imagine how different my colour palette would have been if I had come just two weeks later.

Transylvania is a region in Romania, a country of its own at another time in history, and an example of the fluid maps and ever-changing borders of the world, though the small villages and townspeople have remained much the same for hundreds of years. The second-longest mountain range in Europe, the Carpathian Mountains, provides the backdrop and harbours the largest populations of wolves, brown bears, lynxes and chamois in Romania, as well as the largest area of ancient woodlands in Europe. This is a place of fairytales, horse & carts and medieval villages where you navigate your way with hand-drawn maps past dark faces with moustaches hidden under hats.

Wooden and limed houses with terracotta roofs are washed in a variety of pastels: azure blue, Yellow Monday, sienna, tangerine, magenta, pinks, salmon, soft mustard, dirty green, mint, lichen, sky blue, grey, maroon and lilac. The people who live here do not have much money, but a lot of pride. Much care and effort goes into the appearance of these houses, and a relief detail often displays the date of the build, family crest or a proverb painted in bright colours and mixed with geometric patterns, shields, leaf wreaths and tassels. Grapevine espaliers climb up and over the top of the exteriors, enough to make some wine for the inhabitants.

This softness spoke throughout our travels. A small village, Malancrav means 'little apple' and on the drive towards nearby Apafi Manor, where we were staying, the hillsides were filled with ancient apple orchards – small & organic. An apple press is found in the shed. Inside the manor, floral hand-painted ceramics sit in a mint-coloured library of old linen-covered books and stencilled walls mimic handmade wallpaper. Parties in the evening entertain a handful of guests fireside, a goatskin to sit on & a glass of wine well appreciated after a long day's trail. You wake in the morning to sun streaming in the windows, sunken under linen & lace with the soundscape of cuckoos, and shepherds beating their drums, ringing their bells & cracking their whips to move cattle down the road.

In Transylvania, the palette surrounded me wherever I cast my eyes: hiking in the mountains; the colours of the houses in the villages; amuletic decorations on horses and above doors; the landscape as far as the eye can see, and details of flowers, about to spring into bright, bold colours.

dandelion

librairie

wolf

wildflower

gypsy rose

wildsmen

hellebore

stork's nest

swallowtail

carpathian

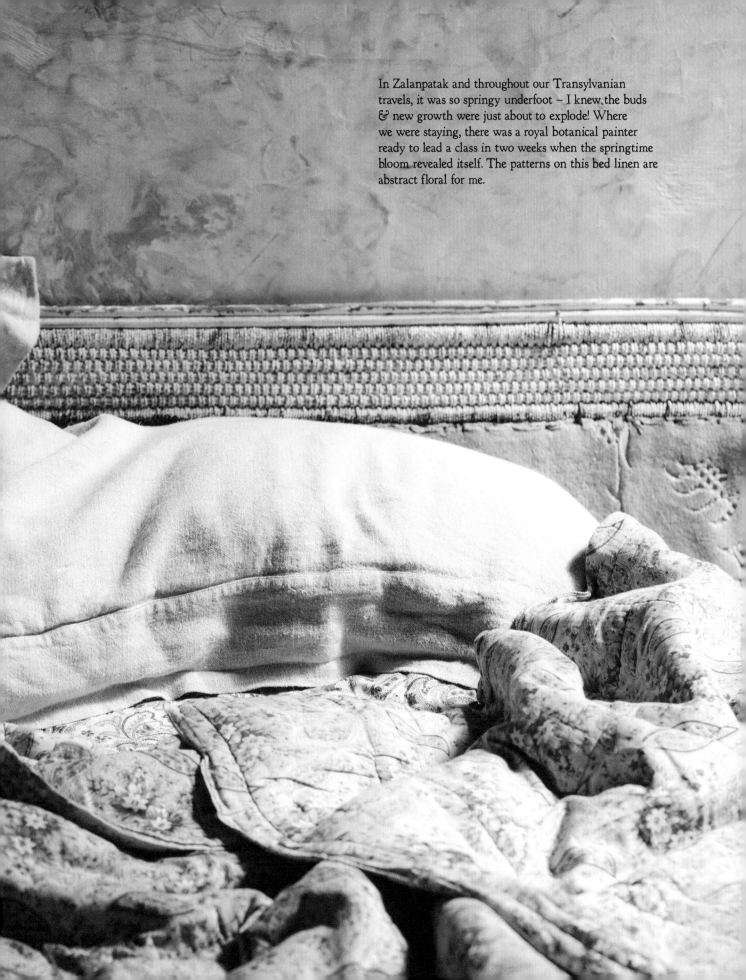

In Zalanpatak and throughout our Transylvanian travels, it was so springy underfoot — I knew the buds & new growth were just about to explode! Where we were staying, there was a royal botanical painter ready to lead a class in two weeks when the springtime bloom revealed itself. The patterns on this bed linen are abstract floral for me.

This is horse-and-cart country where villages are spaced 6–10 miles apart and consist of a church, one road, and houses often with a brightly painted exterior. Internally each house has a yard, a stable for horses, barn for chickens & a kitchen garden for fruit & vegetables. The villagers are forest foragers as well, collecting mushrooms, chestnuts and berries, and tending hives. I find vintage botanical charts at flea markets and hang them as wallpaper.

[PREVIOUS PAGES] Garlic is pinned above all the doorways throughout homes in the villages. Even though it is actually to ward off the evil eye, I prefer to imagine the mythical Dracula being the cause. Have a variation on the theme with something a little more decorative (as opposed to pagan) and pick raffia pompoms to hang from shelves, the backs of doors, cupboard handles or anywhere else you wish. If you line up more than one, it is like make-your-own fringing.

On a warm and cloudless day, we set out from Zalanpatak on a bear hunt. First essential stop was to fill our water bottles at the 100-year-old spring. A hollowed trunk serves as a well with pebbles & stones in the bottom and a wooden lid sitting on top. It is well known that the surrounding Carpathian Mountains and woodlands are filled with bears & wolves. We hear shepherds' whistles herding the ferocious dogs that protect their flocks from these wild animals. We climb higher with hellebores and wild orchids underfoot, and head to a grove of silver birch with spring leaves offering dappled shade for a picnic lunch on the mountainside. Caraway brandy and boiled eggs are on the menu.

[THESE PAGES] The most commonly recognised traditional Transylvanian textiles would have to be in stripes, seen in the tea towels and linen sacks. As well, tiny little flowers are cross-stitched into dresses or bed linen. For some reason these patterns of checks or plaids & florals & stripes now sit together in my mind, the meeting of the utilitarian stripe with the decorative floral.

[PREVIOUS PAGES] These are medieval villages and many are not much changed. The Romanians are ploughing potato patches, ready for seeding by May 1st and the soundscape is filled with bells attached to the working horses. Other background noises are church bells tolling, bees humming, cuckoos and woodpeckers and the clip-clop of horses on roads. The occasional all-purpose tractors are the only motor noise.

On a whim I decide to set up some stills with all the lovely things I can find. Left to our own devices at Apafi Manor, I explore every drawer and cupboard, finding a treasure trove of linens & textiles, porcelain & cutlery. Collect what normally is hidden away and have it at hand for your bed, table or gypsy picnic. You're more likely to dress up your everyday events if you have not forgotten about the insides of the linen cupboard.

[THESE PAGES] Create your own festivities – this fancy is inspired by the mingling of pagan rituals and religious beliefs I witnessed throughout the towns. On a late-afternoon walk we saw pine branches tied with paper streamers hung on church doors, perhaps a celebration or warding off of evil.

Trades of Gypsies

    Silvermakers
Flower sellers
   Tinkers &
Coppersmiths
    Bear leaders
Sievemakers
Horse dealers
Musicians

Zalanpatak was established 400 years ago as a glass manufacturing village. Czechs and Germans were brought in to make glass, & their descendants live on in the area today. We thought it proper to visit the glass museum in light of this history. It was actually just an old couple's home with a table of about ten glass vessels. The main space was broken up into his & her domain: a man's quarters with a workshop and the woman's quarters with the kitchen. The elderly man was in an apron ready to fix or make, and so much more. With his set-up he could turn a wooden bowl, make a harness, repair a hoe, create jewellery and anything else that he was called upon for in order to be self-sufficient. Make your space multi-functional — kitchen as dining room, dining room as workshop, workshop as anything you like.

A missed turn in Transylvania on the way from Miklosvar to Viscri led onto a forest track. Heading NW (or so we hoped), early spring leaves of birch & oak, plum & apple blossom lined the road as we followed a river. We passed some children collecting wild strawberries, a one-armed horse-and-cart driver, some campers with their beers cooling in the stream, many steep cart tracks leading into the higher forest, and a coal-burning camp.

The coal burners set up summer camp on their yearly grounds deep in the forests, building Andy Goldsworthy-esque sculptures of stacked chopped wood in a large circle about 2 metres high and 15 metres wide with a 4 metre high pyramid shape in the middle. This is slow burnt for many days with hay as it slowly turns to charcoal. It is walking back in time, pre-machinery & commercialism.

This is my slightly more glamorous version minus the soot. Create a small fantastical world indoors or out where you can escape to for reading & daydreaming.

My good friend and editor Leta gifted me the fabulous book *Between the Woods and the Water* by Patrick Leigh Fermor before my travels to Romania. I had the pleasure of reading it while I was there. On his own travels through the region, he wrote in a giant notebook that he promptly lost for 50-odd years. It romanticised my journey and I always thought that around the next bend there would be gypsies dancing and hanging their skirts to dry by the river. He met such fantastic people and spent long lazy summer days & nights having parties with gypsy music, falling in love and wandering through the woodlands.

[PREVIOUS PAGES] Other than looking like a fairytale, there is a lot of magic & mysticism surrounding the ancient area of Transylvania. Not only stories of Dracula and the Pied Piper, but I dare say Little Red Riding Hood and Goldilocks & the Three Bears amongst others originated in these areas. We hear of wolves, lynxes & bears in the forests: howling on a winter's night, or dew sipped from the hollow of a bear's footprint, ancient forests of tree nymphs and wood sprites. Display special pieces to conjure up your own version of magic.

[THESE PAGES] Leading up to the villages, on the tops of poles and roofs alike, townspeople create specially placed platforms up high. The storks arrive on March 15th every year to raise their chicks, and leave on August 26th. Because of their giant size, they appear as garlands floating on the peaks of buildings.

Bring your bed outside in summer on the warmer nights. Use a butterfly net to hunt frogs and toads; one of them may turn into a prince if you're lucky.

[PREVIOUS PAGES] My love of linen led me to this setting. I had been buying up some reworked vintage linen from one of my fave stores in NYC, Ochre. I traced them back to their source, a place north of Cluj in Transylvania. Unfortunately for me, my trip fell on Labour Day, May 1st, & I missed my opportunity to visit. I did manage to find some lovely pieces in the places I stayed and in a fortified church perched on higher ground in the medieval village of Viscri.

[THESE PAGES] I encourage you to pick flowers, tendrils or branches from your local surrounds, the garden or the side of the road – whatever they may offer. If you go for flower markets or florists, don't buy a pre-arranged bunch, but many individual flowers and greenery and loosely arrange them together. Imagine you've collected them as you traverse the Transylvanian countryside in the springtime, grouping them as you find them and popping them in vessels once home without another thought.

A highly recommended read if you are visiting Transylvania, or simply want to be transported there from your armchair, is *Along the Enchanted Way* by William Blacker. He talks of gypsy girls with ribbons and shells plaited through their hair and strung around their necks to ward off evil spirits. Create your own protection for your house to ward off the bad and invite the good. I have wrapped raffia around a found antler and hung it alongside threaded cowrie shells and mirrored jingle-jangle from Jaipur, India.

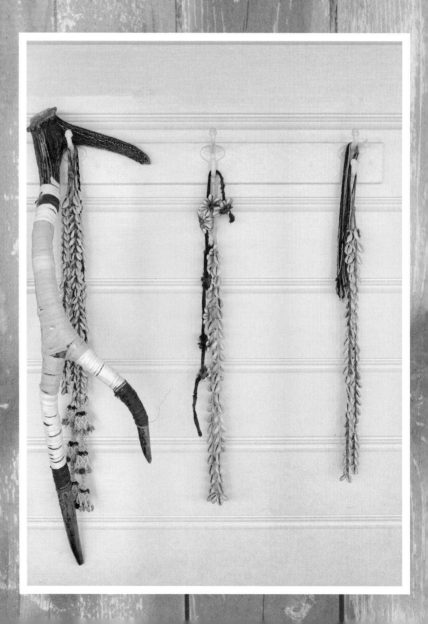

As we travelled, our favourite breakfast became yoghurt with honey, bread & butter and soft-boiled eggs. There is no slow food movement in Transylvania, it's just slow food preserved and made in traditional ways. Gypsies make decorative pressed tin gutters & corners, and other metalwork and this mixture of ceramics with zinc-topped table, brass bells and delicate silver spoons is in homage to the finer details they create, and that add a special moment in a home.

There's a real lack of plastic in Romania. Things are not disposable, they can be mended and fixed and this wear & tear speaks of a lifetime. We wandered past a cracked glass window in a village and rather than being replaced, the owner sewed either side with buttons to keep it from falling apart. Choose your materials carefully when you are buying things, perhaps a little more expensive initially but more likely to live to tell tales.

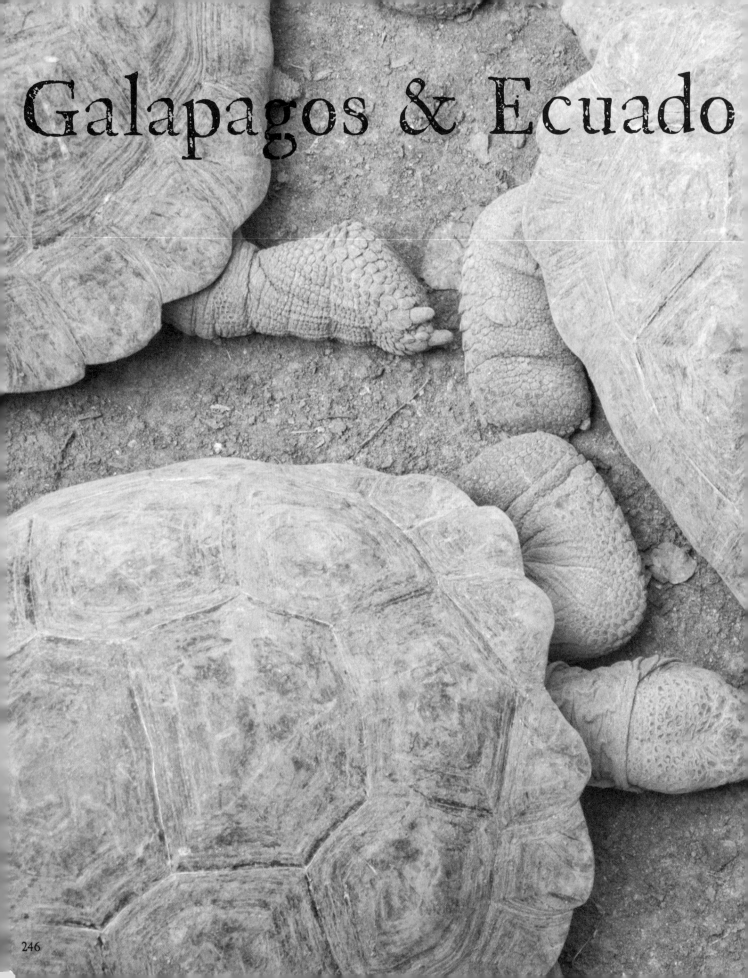

Galapagos & Ecuado

LIBRARY

Plumas: Birds in Ecuador
By Murray Cooper & Rudy Gelis

A Pirate of Exquisite Mind: Explorer, Naturalist & Buccaneer: The Life of William Dampier
By Diana & Michael Preston

On the Origin of Species
By Charles Darwin

TO STAY

Casa Gangotena Hotel
Bolívar Oe6-41 y Cuenca
Quito, Ecuador
www.casagangotena.com

Hacienda San Agustin de Callo
Lasso, Province of Cotopaxi
South of Quito, off the Panamerican Highway
Ecuador
www.incahacienda.com

Hacienda Zuleta
Angochagua
Imbabura Province
Ecuador
www.zuleta.com

Angermeyer Waterfront Inn
Punta Estrada
Puerto Ayora, Santa Cruz Island
Galapagos, Ecuador
www.angermeyer-waterfront-inn.com

Finch Bay Eco Hotel
Puerto Ayora, Santa Cruz Island
Galapagos, Ecuador
www.finchbayhotel.com
I didn't stay here but it was in a great location.

TO SHOP

Homero Ortega
Benalcazar 2-52 y Sucre
Quito, Ecuador
www.homeroortega.com
I'm never without a Panama hat when I travel and often pick them up as I go. I was very excited to choose one from their place of origin!

TO VISIT

Teatro Bolívar
Bolívar Theatre Foundation
Pasaje Espejo 847 y Guayaquil
Centro Histórico de Quito, Ecuador
www.teatrobolivar.org
A burnt-out old theatre – go check it out.

Museo de la Ciudad
Garcia Moreno S1-47 y Rocafuerte
Quito, Ecuador
www.museociudadquito.gob.ec

Calle la Ronda
Quito, Ecuador
This is a beautiful old street with lots going on, wander down it at night time for some empanada & hot chocolate.

St Peter's Bizcocho (biscuit) Factory
Cayambe, Ecuador

La Compania
Benalcazar 562 y Antonio Jose de Sucre
Quito, Ecuador

Otavalo Market
Ave. Amazonas N23-23 y Veintimilla
Otavalo, Imbabura Province
Ecuador

TO EAT/DRINK

Café Dios No Muere
Flores y Junin Esquina N4-10
Quito, Ecuador

Reference

32 Pink embroidered Mexican textile from My Island Home. Coral linen cushions from Cotton Love. Papier-mâché flamingo from The Society inc. Oil painting by my grandmother of Smiths Lake, where she lived.

38 Acapulco chair from Terrace. Hanging orchids from Mr. Cook. Hexagon runner from Armadillo & Co. Vegetable ivory hanging beads on column from the markets of Ecuador. Curtain from Caravane dip-dyed by Shibori the colour of the waters of Galapagos. Twig table found somewhere or other & given a new lease on life with a lick of paint. Photographed at Cockatoo Island.

43 On the daybed, green stripey fabric, hand-loomed in Morocco, from Tiny Bird. Pink cross cushion & green hand-painted linen cushions from Bonnie and Neil. Palm tree print cushion from The Society inc. Pink tape from Pearl Paint NYC (it comes in many sizes & colours & you can write anything you like). Photographed at Brunswick Heads.

46 Vintage print cushions from Homeworks Design Store. Hand-painted vase from Seasonal Concepts. Moroccan teaglasses, coloured plates & jug from Loft. Soft stripey textile from Pure and General, used as tablecloth. Printed linen cushions in Chiang Mai Dragon by Schumacher. Photographed at Pittwater at Peter Lewis of Porter's Paints' place.

51 Pink stripey textile from Tiny Bird. Colourful cross made by Jai from AHOY Trader. Shot at Byron View Farm.

52 Painting by Lydia Balbal from Arthouse Gallery. Flamingo wallpaper from Boyd Blue. Ceramic green parrots from Orson & Blake. Chairs from Le Forge. Flamingo armchair from Arthur G. Old-fashioned Formica-top table and jug from Seasonal Concepts. Towel from Strangetrader. Flowers from Grandiflora. Seagrass matting from the Natural Floorcovering Centre. Photographed at Cockatoo Island.

55 Vixen & Velvet mirror. Roses from Glasshaus. Sink from Izzi & Popo.

58 Bent cane lounge from The Junk Company, covered in one of my mother's unusual suzanis from Central Asia. This textile helped cement the colour palette with its unexpected colour combination. Purple parrot candle from Fenton & Fenton. Rug from Cadrys. Roses from Glasshaus. I found this giant shell at Turnbull Brothers Antiques in Milton.

63 Wicker chair from PAD and rug from Cadrys.

64 Peacock cane chair from PAD. Rug from Cadrys. Shot at Pittwater at Peter Lewis of Porter's Paints' place.

Indochine

ລິກหา.ຊຍງບົງລິເລະ.ນງງແກ່

In Vietnam, it feels like the shops change on a weekly basis. Don't trust that the websites are keeping up with the changes. Check all addresses with your concierge before you head out.

LIBRARY

Cambodia guide:
Kimchen Lach on +(855) 77447133 or kim_angkortour@yahoo.com

Angkor: a photographic portrait
By Jaroslav Poncar

Laos: Sacred Rituals of Luang Prabang
By Hans Georg Berger
www.hansgeorgberger.de

Early Mapping of Southeast Asia
By Thomas Suarez

Liaigre
By Christian Liaigre & Thomas Luntz

Cabinet of Natural Curiosities
By Albertus Seba
Check it out for butterfly inspiration.

TO STAY

Amantaka
55/3 Kingkitsarath Rd
Ban Thongchaleun, Luang Prabang
Laos
www.amanresorts.com/amantaka/home.
aspx

Amansara
Road to Angkor, Siem Reap
Kingdom of Cambodia
www.amanresorts.com/amansara/home.
aspx

The Nam Hai
Hamlet 1 Dien Duong Village
Dien Ban District, Quang Nam Province
Hoi An
Vietnam
www.thenamhai.com

Sofitel Legend Metropole Hanoi
15 Ngo Quyen St
Hoan Kiem District
Hanoi
Vietnam
www.sofitel.com/Hanoi
Stay in the old section.

TO SHOP

Prolung Khmer Pottery & Weaving
Centre
Road to Prasat Bakong, Siem Reap
Cambodia
Tel +855 (0)121759970, +855 (0)12632791
(Khmer)

WA Gallery Concept Store
At Foreign Correspondent Club Angkor
Hotel
Pokambor Ave (next to the Royal
Residence)
Siem Reap
Cambodia
www.fcccambodia.com

Caruso Lao Home Craft
60 Sakaline Rd
Luang Prabang
Laos
www.carusolao.com

L'usine Le Loi
70B Le Loi St
District 1
Saigon
Vietnam
www.lusinespace.com

Tan My
61 Hang Gai St
Hoan Kiem District
Hanoi
Vietnam
www.tanmydesign.com

Le Cong Kieu St
District 1 (access from Ben Thanh
Market)
Saigon
Vietnam
An entire street of antique shops.

Song
75 Pasteur St, District 1
65 Le Loi St, Saigon Centre, District 1
63 Pasteur St, District 1
Parkson Saigon Tourist, Dong Khoi,
District 1
Saigon
Vietnam
www.asiasongdesign.com

TO VISIT

Reunification Palace
106 Nguyen Du St
District 1
Saigon
Vietnam
www.dinhdoclap.gov.vn

Botanical Gardens (& zoo)
2 Nguyen Binh Khiem St
District 1
Saigon
Vietnam

Magic waterfalls
Phnom Kulen National Park
Siem Reap
Cambodia

Reclining Buddha of Preah Ang Thom
Phnom Kulen National Park
Siem Reap
Cambodia

Daily Morning Market
Alleys between Main St. (Sisavangvong Rd)
& Mekong River
Luang Prabang
Laos

Royal Palace Museum
Sisavangvong Rd
Luang Prabang
Laos

TO EAT/DRINK

Miss Wong Cocktail Bar
The Lane, Between Hospital St & St 11
Siem Reap
Cambodia

Le Banneton Café
46 Sakkhaline Rd
Luang Prabang
Laos

Temple Club
29-31 Ton That Thiep St
District 1
Saigon
Vietnam
www.templeclub.com.vn

Foreign Correspondent Club Angkor
Restaurant & Bar
Pokambor Ave (next to the Royal
Residence)
Siem Reap
Cambodia
www.fcccambodia.com

Nha Hang Ngon
160 Pasteur St
District 1
Saigon
Vietnam

L'Usine
151/1 Dong Khoi St
1st floor
District 1
Saigon
Vietnam
www.lusinespace.com

Cong Caphe
152D Trieu Viet Vuong, Hai Ba Trung
32 Dien Bien Phu, Ba Dinh
Hanoi
Vietnam
www.congcaphe.com

Hanoi Social Club
6 Hoi Vu, Hoan Kiem
Hanoi
Vietnam

Reference

72 Orange folding chairs from Water Tiger. Leather piano straps & a bamboo pole are rigged to create a hanging device for showing off beautiful bed linen. This becomes a great screening system, and you can rotate your textiles. From left to right: a silk ochre piece stitched so finely together in panels, a beautiful example of Korean pojagi patchwork bought years ago from Sri in New York. A scarf length, crocheted diamond piece found at Longbarn in Braidwood NSW, sits next to an old wire bicycle basket, used to store pegs or anything else you like, from The Junk Company in Melbourne. Two old Kantha blankets in lovely patterns from my bestie Sally Campbell who I travel regularly with to India. She designs her own range of bed linen, scarves and clothes & works tirelessly with weavers, master dyers, quilters & embroiderers all over. Find her through Sally Campbell Textiles. Lastly, a collaboration of Sydneysiders: lovely natural linen strips knitted by Little Dandelion then over-dyed by Karen & Pepa of Shibori. I pick up industrial lights at auction & weekend fossicking, and always have a stash at the ready. Shot at Cockatoo Island.

75 Chalkboard cloth from Me Too Please which deals in Mexican oilcloth and has every pattern under the sun. Old wooden cinema seating and red industrial light from Vixen & Velvet – great for a hallway! Woven chicken basket used as a pendant lamp from Fenton & Fenton. Shot at Establishment Studios.

76 Large metal pan from Water Tiger used as catchment in a wet room. Linen curtain from Secret River. I look for external bathroom fixtures regularly in flea markets & salvage shops – the more patina the better. Hand-knotted bait bag found at Dosa in NYC, a great way of storing your soap because you can get them wet, just like the fishermen who use them.

81 Wooden trestle table & folding chairs from Water Tiger. A silk ochre textile goes from hanger to tablecloth and is strewn with mismatched porcelain by Mud Australia and a brass lassi vessel from Garden Life. Never be shy to add non-functional

but interesting finds to your tea or Pho party. I have a thing for tassels & amulets, and picked up this tassel in Istanbul's Arasta Bazaar when hunting for textiles. Shot at Cockatoo Island.

84 A still-life of old & new. I love lotus season – these ones are from Grandiflora. I have been working with Saskia for 20 years & I call on her for all special flora. She created the magic world for my mum's funeral & we danced in the church to Leonard Cohen's 'Dance Me to the End of Love' as the flowers were arranged. I pick up bits 'n' bobs throughout my travels, the dip-dyed horsehair keychain was bought for my assistant Hannah from General Store, Venice Beach, and the cicada box was my mother's, carved from bone from India.

87 Folding wooden table from Water Tiger. Woven wicker light from Bisque. A gift from my beautiful assistants, a campaign chair from Tarlo & Graham for my 40th. Rug from Armadillo & Co. Metal urn & lassi cup from Garden Life.

90 You can get these mats everywhere, I grabbed mine from local markets. Wooden beaded lights from Marz Designs. White organdie-pieced curtain from Sally Campbell Textiles. Daybed from Water Tiger.

92 I love the snake puppet on the wall, from Fenton & Fenton. Linens include yellow sheets from Mark Tuckey, natural pillowcases from Izzi & Popo, bolsters made from duffel bags bought at Porte de Clignancourt. Lucky for me it was peony season and I got these from Glasshaus.

95 Hand-painted horse from Water Tiger. Brass vessel from Garden Life. African reed & leather mat from Kulchi.

96 Chairs from The Junk Company. Fireplace from Oblica. Light from Christopher Boots. Shot on location at Oblica showroom.

97 Utilise a great background and layer it with a light hand. Globe from The Junk Company and painted tree stump from Mark Tuckey make for a cultural still-life. Shot at the Oblica showroom.

99 I've used a geometric modern chair and chevron rug from Fenton & Fenton and added some retro headphones from The Junk Company. Light, stool and butcher's block all from The Junk Company. Handmade charcoal, crumpled wallpaper drop designed by Matthew Collins from Art & Interiors. You don't even need to cover the wall, just create a focal point with one beautiful drop. I picked up the cast-metal mosquito coil that hangs so elegantly from its purpose-made hook at Analogue Life while travelling in Japan with my assistants.

103 Dip-dyed saffron curtain panel by Shibori. Baskets from Fenton & Fenton. Vintage Kantha lampshade from The Society inc. This interior works because of the combination of soft and hard surfaces. It is also a good consideration for sound in a space.

104 Vixen & Velvet charcoal daisy pendant made from wooden beads, and leather cat mask from Love, Adorned in New York.

106 Indian calligraphy books from Vixen & Velvet. I can never have too many scissors; these are handmade from Vietnam, next to hand-forged nails. A beautiful dustpan made out of cardboard rubbed with pomegranate juice from Japan. A wallpaper brush picked up somewhere along the way.

110 Knitted linen throw from Little Dandelion, vintage Kantha quilt and cushion from Sally Campbell Textiles. Linen sheets from Honeybee Homewares, printed linen cloth used as a bedhead from Sixhands. You can create a defined space simply through hanging cloth; in this interior it anchors a bed.

Turkey

LIBRARY

Cornucopia magazine
www.cornucopia.net
Buy at the airport for great articles

Portrait of a Turkish Family
By Irfan Orga

Bodrum guide: Don Frey
www.amphoras.com
A physicist by trade, shipwreck diver & treasure
hunter by passion – a wealth of info & enthusiasm.

TO STAY

Macakizi Hotel
Kesire Mevkii, Narcicegi Sok.
Golturkbuku
Near Bodrum, Turkey
www.macakizi.com

Hotel Empress Zoe
Akbiyik Cad. No. 10
Sultanahmet
Istanbul, Turkey
www.emzoe.com

The House Hotel
Galatasaray
Firuzaga Mah. Bostanbasi Cad. No. 19
Beyoglu
Istanbul, Turkey
www.thehousehotel.com

TO SHOP

Grand Bazaar
Istanbul, Turkey

My fave stores:

Dervis
Kapalicarsi, Keseciler Cad., No.33-35 and Halicilar Cad.,
No.51
www.dervis.com
I stopped here briefly on the first day but went back
with more time on my last day. The longer you stay,
the more you find. Passionate owners (they have
2 stores & a few brothers) find old dowry pieces
amongst many other textiles, mostly from Turkey but
some from India too, and have a great selection. Some
more precious than others, but my love is for the more
naïve, understated nomadic ones. They have bolts of
old hammam linen, Turkish towels, woven jute, sacks,
blankets and all the new hammam towels as well. I
bought tassled everything: woollen blankets, hand-
beaten hammam bowls, dowry tea towels and other
must-haves that I left with them to kindly ship home.

Yazzma
Kapali Carsi Takkeciler Sok. No. 58-60
www.yazzma.com
New by-the-yard ikat lengths in silk, cotton and velvet.
I am crazy about dots & zig-zags at the moment. So
after about an hour of pulling everything off the
shelves, decisions were made. The fabric is folded so
neatly and concisely. It is mind-blowing. They have
ready-made cushion covers & bolsters, an easy suitcase
pack!

Horasan
Yorgancilar Cad. No. 22.
If, like me, you love talismans & amulets and other
jingle-jangle, this store is chock-a-block full of all your
needs. Tassels, beads, coins, bells, ready-made stuff: it's
all here.

Arasta Bazaar
Arasta Carsisi No. 143
Sultanahmet
Istanbul, Turkey
www.arastabazaar.com
The best place for antique textiles in here is Motif
Nomadic Art at No. 77.

Hazal Kilim
Mecidiyekoy Koprusu Sokak No. 9
Ortakoy, Turkey
www.hazalkilim.com
For rugs.

Mehmet Cetinkaya Gallery
Kucuk Ayasofya Cad.
Tavukhane Sokak No. 7
Sultanahmet
Istanbul, Turkey
www.cetinkayagallery.com

TO VISIT

The Bodrum Museum of Underwater Archaeology
Carsi Mh.
Bodrum, Mugla Province
Turkey
www.bodrum-museum.com

The Museum of Innocence
Cukurcuma Cad., Dalgic Cikmazi 2
Beyoglu
Istanbul, Turkey
www.masumiyetmuzesi.org

Gumusluk, Turkey
A small fishing port & village with a weekly artisan
market, seaside dining and trips to the nearby ghost
town.

Divan Literature Museum
Galip Dede Cad No. 15
Tunel, Beyoglu
Istanbul

TO DO

Southern Cross Blue Cruising
www.southerncrossbluecruising.com
Spend a day out on a gulet from Bodrum.

Cagaloglu Hammam
Cagaloglu, Istanbul
www.cagalogluhamami.com.tr

TO EAT/DRINK

Denizhan
Ataturk Bulvari No. 275
Konacik, Bodrum
Turkey
www.denizhan.com
The mezze is delicious local cheese, handmade butter
& all fruit and vegetables from the owner's own
farm which is visible from the outdoor terrace. We
had heard it's the best place for lamb skewers (it is!)
wrapped in pita-like bread, served in pieces with local
thick yoghurt & a selection of four dried herbs &
spices, grilled tomato & peppers. Note: try not to fill
up on the mezze and leave room for the kebab.

Lokanta Maya
Kemankes Cad. 35A
Karakoy, Istanbul
Turkey
www.lokantamaya.com

Karakoy Lokantasi
Kemankes Cad. 37A
Karakoy, Istanbul
Turkey
www.karakoylokantasi.com

Istanbul Modern
Meclis-i Mebusan Cad. Liman Isletmeleri Sahasi
Antrepo No:4
Karakoy, Istanbul
Turkey
www.istanbulmodern.org/en
The cafe at the gallery of modern art is fab, stunning
views and right on the Bosphorus.

Reference

118 Use cane furniture that can go indoors & out from Lincoln Brooks. I cut up a couple of old canvas sails and reworked them to use as a rug that sits slightly askew. Continue the romance of lounging around on a sailboat with a dyed, woven beanbag from Koskela. Splattered water cushion from Bonnie and neil and Shibori dip-dyed knitted piece from Little Dandelion used as a window treatment. Bowls on coffee table from Katie Watson Ceramics. Red & white stacking chair from Le Forge. Shot at Cockatoo Island.

121 Spotted tablecloth from Sally Campbell Textiles. The wooden lid of a Vincent Van Duysen vessel used as a trivet for Katie Watson Ceramics evil eye plate. Porcelain fortune cookies from The Society inc. Porcelain spoon with indigo inlay from Mociun and an exotic parrot feather that was a gift for my birthday from Sally Campbell.

122 Moulded aluminium spoons from my fave shop in Ibiza, Sluiz. In Turkey you normally find evil eyes in glass but here it is in resin, a keepsake from a Dinosaur Designs party in Sydney, and a cloth strainer from Vietnam.

123 Vixen & Velvet table.

126 Quilt & cushions by Sally Campbell Textiles. Fabric light from The Society inc. Rug from Armadillo & Co. Ercol bench from Temperature. Red & white chair from Le Forge.

128 Mosquito net & rope dip-dyed by Shibori. Cushion from AHOY Trader. Draughts board from Heath's Old Wares. Shot at La Casa Artist Residency in Byron Bay.

131 White porcelain platter from Mud Australia. Katie Watson Ceramic cups.

133 Chair and sailing ship painting from Fabulous Mrs Fox. Anchor & arrows on the wall from Three Potato Four. Dyed ropes by Shibori coiled in circles just as they were on the decks of boats in Turkey. Shot at La Casa Artist Residency in Byron Bay.

134 Blue metal folding chairs from Water Tiger. Spotted tablecloth from Sally Campbell Textiles. Stripey scarf from Strangetrader. Evil eye porcelain from Katie Watson Ceramics. Vincent Van Duysen vessels from Hub. Glass drink dispenser from The Society inc.

138 Shot at The Pines, Manly.

147 Cane outdoor chair from The Junk Company. Blue camo oilcloth from Me Too Please. Hexagon dhurrie from Fenton & Fenton. Deck sail beanbag and wooden bunting from Mark Tuckey.

148 Wooden trunk from Vixen & Velvet. Orange linen sheet by Bedouin Societe from Mark Tuckey. Shibori throw from Sluiz in Ibiza. I bought these old cast-iron gaming numbers from artist David Bromley. Shot at Establishment Studios.

149 Seamen painted on glass vessels by Hunter Amos (11-year-old genius artist, sometimes available from Atlantic, Byron Bay). Shot at Byron View Farm.

150 The terracotta with white glaze detail by Joost are ready for a lunchtime feast. These lovely wooden spoons from Sluiz, Ibiza, were hand carved out of soft wood, perfect for serving & sharing. A large enamel pitcher from my own shop, The Society inc. Piet Hein Eek Scrapwood wallpaper sets the tone of a beachside shack. Hanging compass was forged and tinkered by Coloforge.

Scotland

LIBRARY

Alastair Sawday's
www.sawdays.co.uk
Great travel guide, especially for B&B's.

Bird Hand Book
By Victor Schrager & A. S. Byatt

Pictures
By Tim Walker

TO STAY

Bramble Bield
Powis House
Stirling FK9 5PS
Scotland
www.bramblebield.com

Applecross Inn
Applecross
Wester Ross IV54 8LR
Scotland
www.applecross.uk.com/inn

Drover's Inn
Inverarnan
North Loch Lomond G83 7DX
Scotland
www.thedroversinn.co.uk

Strongarbh House
Tobermory
Isle of Mull PA75 6PR
Scotland
www.strongarbh.com

Glengarry Castle Hotel
Invergarry
Inverness-shire PH35 4HW
Scotland
www.glengarry.net

TO SHOP

Unicorn Antiques
65 Dundas St
Edinburgh EH3 6RS
Scotland
www.unicornantiques.co.uk

21st Century Kilts
48 Thistle St
Edinburgh EH2 1EN
Scotland
www.21stcenturykilts.com

IJ Mellis Cheesemonger
30a Victoria St,
Edinburgh EH1 2JW
Scotland
www.mellischeese.net

Papa Stour
www.papastour.com
Amazing craft & design online and
stay in their beautiful holiday cottage in
Callakille, Applecross.

AG Hendy Home Store
36 High St
Hastings
East Sussex TN34 3ER
England
www.homestore-hastings.co.uk
If you can – a must-visit in the south of
the United Kingdom.

TO VISIT

Jupiter Artland
Bonnington House Steadings
Wilkieston
Edinburgh EH27 8BB
Scotland
www.jupiterartland.org

Inverewe Garden & Estate
Poolewe
Ross-shire IV22 2LG
Scotland
www.nts.org.uk/Property/Inverewe-
Garden-Estate

Tobermory Distillery
Ledaig
Tobermory
Isle of Mull PA75 6NR
Scotland
www.tobermorymalt.com
Book for tour to avoid disappointment.

Duart Castle
Isle of Mull
Argyll PA64 6AP
Scotland
www.duartcastle.com

Iona Abbey
Isle of Iona
Argyll PA76 6SQ
Scotland

Drummond Castle Gardens
Muthill
Crieff PH7 4HZ
Scotland
www.drummondcastlegardens.co.uk

Glenlyon Tweed Mill
Taybridge Terrace, Aberfeldy
Perthshire PH15 2BS
Scotland
www.glenlyontweedmill.com

Ardalanish
Isle of Mull Weavers
Bunessan
Isle of Mull PA67 6DR
www.ardalanish.com

Edinburgh Farmers' Market
Castle Terrace
Edinburgh EH1 2EL
Scotland
www.edinburghfarmersmarket.com
Every Saturday 9am – 2pm.

Charleston
Firle, Lewes
East Sussex BN8 6LL
England
www.charleston.org.uk
If you're in the south of England, don't
miss the Bloomsbury Group's country
meeting place.

TO EAT/DRINK

Café Fish
15 North West Circus Place
Edinburgh EH3 6SX
Scotland
www.cafefish.net

Timberyard
10 Lady Lawson St
Edinburgh EH3 9DS
Scotland
www.timberyard.co

Ninth Wave Restaurant
Bruach Mhor
Fionnphort
Isle of Mull PA66 6BL
Scotland
www.ninthwaverestaurant.co.uk
Be sure to book.

Love Crumbs
155 West Port
Edinburgh EH3 9DP
Scotland
www.lovecrumbs.co.uk
A recommendation from Timberyard.

Urban Angel
1 Forth St
Edinburgh EH1 3JX
www.urban-angel.co.uk
Sobering coffee & almond/orange cake.

The Bon Vivant
55 Thistle St
Edinburgh
Scotland EH2 1DY
www.bonvivantedinburgh.co.uk

Reference

158 Bed linen and beautiful flatware & tableware from Izzi & Popo. Cushions & throw from Tigger Hall Design. Scout hat from Chapel St Bazaar in Melbourne. Flowers and plants from Glasshaus. Shot at Establishment Studios.

161 Perforated metal container from Tarlo & Graham. Plants from Glasshaus. Shot at Establishment Studios.

170 Plants from Glasshaus. Log in disguise from Nyary. Shot at Establishment Studios.

172 Society bed linen from Ondene. The tent is made out of blankets I bought in Ecuador. Shot at the Greengate Hotel, room designed by Kelly Ross of The Gentry.

175 Tableware and flatware from Izzi & Popo. Horn beakers bought in Ibiza. Shot at Establishment Studios.

176 Chippendale chairs & ottoman by Edit. Prickly Pear from Mr Cook and felted oversized knit throw by Little Dandelion.

178 Old tin box and antlers from Seasonal Concepts. Rope brush gift from amazing florist, Phil.

180 Cane covered vessel from Seasonal Concepts. Shot at the Beresford Hotel in Sydney.

184 Flowers from Glasshaus. Painting from Unicorn Antiques in Scotland.

187 A display of Scottish-like pieces. Antler & frames from Seasonal Concepts. Hooks made by my talented blacksmith, Saul. Additional bits 'n' bobs from The Society inc.

190 Bench and stool from Mark Tuckey. Light from The Junk Company. My own blanket bought at Maiwa in Canada. Shot at Oblica Showroom.

192 Floor canvas and pillow from Pony Rider. Antlers from Seasonal Concepts. Shot at William and Jo White's house, above their shop Fabulous Mrs Fox.

Transylvania

LIBRARY

Between the Woods and the Water
By Patrick Leigh Fermor

Along the Enchanted Way
By William Blacker

Mrs. Delany & Her Circle
Edited by Mark Laird & Alicia Weisberg-Roberts

Time of the Gypsies film
Directed by Emir Kusturica

La Strada film
Directed by Federico Fellini

Underground film & soundtrack
Directed by Emir Kusturica

Wild Flowers of the World
By Barbara Everard & Brian D. Morley

Romania: A Birdwatching and Wildlife Guide
By James Roberts

The Night Circus
By Erin Morgenstern

TO SHOP

Bellocq
37 Greenpoint Ave
Brooklyn 11222
(entrance at 104 West St)
www.bellocq.com
Amazing teas that transport you to far-off places. Choose
one with early spring mixes of delicate orange blossom
and garlands of marigold petals.

TO STAY

The Mihai Eminescu Trust
Malancrav, Romania
www.mihaieminescutrust.org
For homestays and historic houses rentals. The trust rescues
crumbling ancient buildings large & small – I stayed at the Apafi
Manor.

Count Kalnoky's Estate
Zalanpatak no. 1-2, Romania
Miklosvar no. 186-187, Romania
www.transylvaniancastle.com
I stayed at properties in Zalanpatak and Miklosvar, but there are
more.

TO VISIT

Museum of Zoology
Clinicolor St, no. 5-7
Cluj-Napoca, Romania
www.ubbcluj.ro/en/structura/muzee/muzeul_zoologic

Pharmaceutical Museum
Union Square, no. 28 (corner of King Ferdinand)
Cluj-Napoca
Romania
www.muzeulfarmaciei.ro

Reference

204 Printed linen cushion from Tigger Hall Design. Vintage floral quilts, a collection of stylist Glen Proebstel. Shot at Establishment Studios.

208 Botanical prints from The Junk Company. Rorschach inky fabric and cushion from Tigger Hall Design. Perforated metal container from Tarlo & Graham. Wallpaper designed by Matthew Collins from Art & Interiors used on the floor. Sibella's own cotton net curtains hanging on the wall. Shot at Establishment Studios.

210 Raffia pompoms & tassels from AHOY Trader.

211 String ball birch from Glasshaus. Wooden worry beads with horsehair tassel from Fredericks & Mae. Shot at Establishment Studios.

212 Couch from Fabulous Mrs Fox, where this was shot. My own blankets from India.

216 Gypsy bells from The Society inc. Little Dandelion rug.

217 Stripey quilt & green patterned quilt from Sally Campbell Textiles. All other things found by me around the world. Shot at Cockatoo Island.

218 Paper streamers from Confetti System. Rose glasses from Resould in Brunswick Heads. Kantha quilt from Jaipur, India. Shot on location at William and Jo White's house, above Fabulous Mrs Fox.

224 Table & enamel jugs from Seasonal Concepts. Chair from French Country available through Julie Lewis Agency. Hide from NSW Leather. Rug from Cadrys. Arrows from Fredericks & Mae. Cabinets from Water Tiger. Beaded chandelier from Coastal Lighting Designs.

228 Scissors from The Society inc. Flowers from Andrea Duff's garden at Byron View Farm.

230 Bathing tent bought at *The Great Gatsby* movie prop sale. Cane daybed bought at auction. Cushions by Walter-G. Grey linen knitted throw by Little Dandelion. Quilts by Sally Campbell Textiles.

234 Bits 'n' bobs borrowed from Andrea Duff of Strangetrader.

237 Floor canvas from Pony Rider and oversized metal net from Fabulous Mrs Fox.

240 Pillowcase & tasseled textiles from Dervis, Keseciler Cad., no.33-35 and Halicilar Cad., no.51 at the Grand Bazaar in Istanbul. Blanket bought at Maiwa in Canada. Stacks of metal trunks from Vixen & Velvet. Polish pajaki paper chandelier from The Society inc.

241 Shot on location at Byron View Farm.

242 Antler from Seasonal Concepts. Shot at Byron View Farm.

243 Handmade arrows from Fredericks & Mae.

245 Grey dinner plates from Mud Australia. Zinc topped table from Seasonal Concepts. Hand-painted scalloped plates bought at French General, many moons ago. Pompom & tasseled textiles from Porte de Vanves Marché in Paris. Compasses & enamel watering can bought at a country auction. Fine silver spoons from Analogue Life in Nagoya, Japan. Porcelain jug with silver lining from ABC Home. Shot at Cockatoo Island.

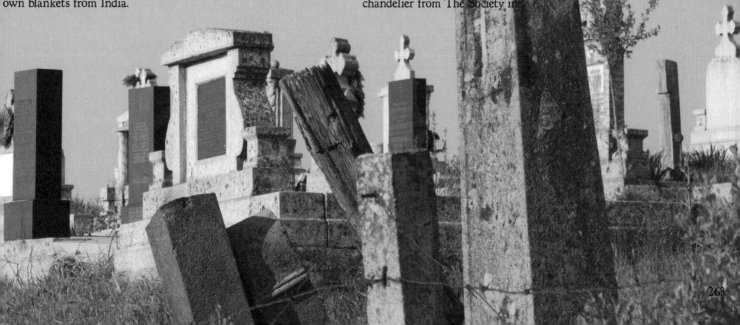

Locations

BYRON VIEW FARM

Andrea Duff & I have been friends for a long time. She was a fashion stylist in New York when I lived there and is the reason I only wear a neutral palette. We were shooting in Central Park for a magazine, and she was styling it and I was the stand-in model/interior stylist. She put me in caramels and creams and told me those colours made me shine and I should consider wearing only them. I never used to wear a lot of bright colours anyway, but gradually cut them all out of my wardrobe.

Nowadays, she and her partner, Robert Schwamberg spend a few months a year sailing in Europe, and collect things for Strangetrader from the ports they visit – textiles, modern bits 'n' bobs mixed with old pieces. She looks at the world in a different way – she might find a piece and dye it, take it in or embellish it in some way.

It's how she's approached Byron View Farm, it's all very unexpected. She and Robert live in the main house which is about 100 years old, and built Byron View a couple of years ago to rent out to visitors (my home away from home). It doesn't feel like a new place at all with its verandahs on four sides, doors everywhere to catch the cross breezes and a garden full of salvias, frangipani, maples, spider lilies, lots of gums, giant bamboo and blackboys by Richard from Garden Life. I picked a lot from it to use in the shoots. They have a mini-orchard and a vegetable garden. Andrea makes the best chicken roast with veges that have just been picked.

When I'm there I hardly ever want to get down from the top of the mountain – I'm quite happy watching the belted Galloways from the verandah, looking at Byron from afar, or enjoying the insane sunsets you get up there.

FABULOUS MRS FOX

William and Jo White are real live tinkers – or tinkerers anyway. They built their shop, Fabulous Mrs Fox, out of salvage and live upstairs. Fabulous Mrs Fox sells lighting William makes – he's a bit of an inventor – plus flea-market finds, books, a crystal ship chandelier I want to buy, and all sorts of other objets. He also makes a nice line of drainpipes in his very cool shed out the back. I love a good drainpipe, so we discussed them a lot while I was there.

William and Jo lived in South Carolina and Argentina for years – their place feels like the coolest apartment in Buenos Aires with its beautifully proportioned rooms, panelled dados, shutters and floorboards, and always a vista to inspire curiosity of what the next room might be.

They made bath plugs for years – when I started out as a stylist in my twenties, I featured those plugs in lots of magazines and newspapers, and had no idea that, years later, I'd meet the people who designed them.

William and Jo let us shoot for the book at the last minute – we'd only just met and they weren't on our itinerary but they became such a key part of the book, and I'm glad I discovered them.

LA CASA ARTIST RESIDENCY

I'd heard about this residency at Belongil that gives artists and musicians space to dream, and a bed for the night – my brother Chris stayed here while we were using it as a location. It's surrounded by pandanus, with a big wraparound verandah and is right on the edge of the water – the sea virtually laps around the floorboards, so you have the feeling that it might disappear one day, which makes it feel even more special.

The residency is a house over two levels with surfboards everywhere, two bedrooms upstairs, and downstairs a kitchen with a fridge full of beer, and a recording studio. We weren't using the studio for our shoot, so requested some music and had the band Mt Warning supply the background tunes to set the mood.

PETER LEWIS'S PLACE

I'd had photos of this boathouse for years, knew where it was, but had no idea who owned it. It turned out to be Peter Lewis of Porter's Paints which should have been obvious due to the distinct colours the walls were painted in – perfect for Galapagos.

The day of the shoot Sydney had the highest rainfall it had ever had, and was blowing a gale – the rain was horizontal, and walking down through the bamboo forest to get to the boathouse was like walking through rain on rain. It didn't matter – the place was ideal with its little group of dwellings, and I can imagine spending a whole summer there.

THE ESTABLISHMENT STUDIOS

Glen Proebstel is one of the best stylists in the world – I was first aware of him when I lived in New York and he was working in Australia, so admired him from afar. His studio in Melbourne is an old warehouse and variety of small rooms, and the people who run it are fantastic. It was so good to have access to all his props and furniture, and one of the reasons I wanted to shoot down in Melbourne was to be able to use all our favourite Melbourne suppliers and give the book a different feel. There's a shift in aesthetic down there – it's not a beach culture like Sydney but is still essentially Australian. The advantage of using a studio is that it gave me the freedom and ability to get the bigger interior shots I wanted for the book.

CHRISTOPHER BOOTS' WORKSHOP

Christopher's workshop is out the back of the Oblica showroom in Fitzroy. I walked through the fireplace showroom, saw Christopher's space and asked him if we could shoot in there. He said yes, and away we went – it was one of those hundred-degree Melbourne days. His lights are glamorous and use materials of copper, brass and quartz. They are more sculptures than lights, works of art that look just as good off as on.

COCKATOO ISLAND

Cockatoo Island is an old defunct shipping yard on an island in Sydney Harbour. The first buildings on the island served as a convict gaol and it's had many reincarnations since 1839, including workshops and service for the Navy, a girls' industrial school, and the building of Australia's first steel warships in the dockyard to name a few. The spaces are high and wide to make way for all the industrial work and a dream for shooting!
The island has so many layers of history. At many other historical locations, these layers stop in time at one point – but here they continue. It is now used as a location for art fairs, dirt bike tracks, film festivals, movies, residential rentals, camping, parties and so much more. Remnants of their presence are left to be embraced and celebrated, and added to its appeal. After last year's biennale I thought this would be a perfect location for *Gypsy*. With the aid of a 4-tonne truck & hired barge, we were deposited on the island for the week with props, furniture, flowers, rigging & the rest. An old warehouse was our holding space & we shot in over 15 locations throughout the island (with the kind loan of golf carts & smaller trucks). I always shoot a large portion of my books in January,

and this year the temperature reached new heights, a 100-year heat record! The amazing Cockatoo Island team also let me experience the magic & romance of camping in Sydney Harbour in the summertime. The cluster of tents on the western side of the island offer everything you need for some serious glamping & waking up at dawn to see the sun rise over the Harbour Bridge was magnificent.

THE PINES

My design for The Pines in Manly, Sydney emerged as a social hangout: part surfclub, part lodge. I wanted to create a relaxed environment to lounge around in, where there are ping-pong tables, surfboards & every other water-related toy stashed nearby & the stories of the day can be exchanged over a game & a drink.
With a revisit to string art and a colour palette that matched Turkey, it offered itself perfectly to *Gypsy*. Every single weekend as a teen, I frequented North Steyne, where the boys surfed in their faded okanuis and we lay about under the giant pines that line the beach.
All my interiors, whether in my home or commercial spaces, are stories of my own experiences, inspired and translated into a physical medium.

THE GREENGATE

My good friend Kelly Ross of The Gentry designed The Terrace Room at the Greengate Hotel in Killara, Sydney. I call it the jungle room – a private dining room with beautiful walls hand-painted in tropical leaves. Fit for adventurers or perhaps the learned members of the Lunar Society a few hundred years ago. Kelly is extremely talented and always creates magical spaces and venues.

Resources

AUSTRALIA

SYDNEY
Armadillo & Co. / www.armadillo-co.com
Atolyia / www.atolyia.com
Cadrys / www.cadrys.com.au
Coastal Lighting Designs / www.coastallightingdesigns.com.au
(through Julie Lewis Agency)
Dinosaur Designs / www.dinosaurdesigns.com.au
Edit / www.edit-group.com.au
Garden Life / www.gardenlife.com.au
Grandiflora / www.grandiflora.net
Honeybee Homewares / www.honeybeehomewares.com.au
Jason Mowen / www.jasonmowen.com
Julie Lewis Agency / www.julielewisagency.net
Katie Watson Ceramics / homedog@bigpond.net.au
Koskela / www.koskela.com.au
Kulchi / www.kulchi.com
Le Forge / www.leforge.com.au
Lincoln Brooks / www.lincolnbrooks.com
Little Dandelion / www.littledandelion.com
Mark Tuckey / www.marktuckey.com.au
Marz Designs / www.marzdesigns.com
Me Too Please / www.metooplease.com.au
Mr Cook / www.mrcook.com.au
Mud Australia / www.mudaustralia.com
NSW Leather / www.leatherco.com.au
Ondene / www.ondene.com.au
Pony Rider / www.ponyrider.com.au

Sally Campbell Textiles / www.sallycampbell.com.au
Seasonal Concepts / www.seasonalconcepts.com.au
Secret River / www.secretriver.com
Shibori / www.shibori.com.au
Signcutters / www.signcutters.com.au
Sixhands / www.sixhands.com.au
The Society inc. / www.thesocietyinc.com.au
Temperature / www.temperaturedesign.com.au
Walter-G / www.walter-g.com.au
Water Tiger / www.watertiger.com.au
Bisque / www.bisqueinteriors.com.au
(through Julie Lewis Agency)

OUT OF SYDNEY
AHOY Trader / www.ahoytrader.com
Fabulous Mrs Fox / 10 Park St, Brunswick Heads NSW 2483
Ginger & Gilligan / www.gingerandgilligan.com
Ha'veli / www.haveli.net.au
Heath's Old Wares / www.heathsoldwares.com.au
Longbarn / www.longbarn.com.au
Polish / www.polishatbyron.com
Racket / www.racket.net.au
Resould / www.resould.com.au
Strangetrader / www.strangetrader.com

MELBOURNE
Art & Interiors / www.artandinteriors.com.au
Bedouin Societe / www.bedouinsociete.com
Bonnie and neil / www.bonnieandneil.com.au

Chapel St Bazaar / 217 Chapel St, Prahran 3181
Christopher Boots / www.christopherboots.com
David Bromley / www.davidbromley.com.au
Fenton & Fenton / www.fentonandfenton.com.au
Glasshaus / www.glasshaus.com.au
Izzi & Popo / www.izziandpopo.com.au
Joost / www.byjoost.com
The Junk Company / www.thejunkcompany.com.au
Mark Tuckey / www.marktuckey.com.au
Nyary / www.nyary.com.au
Oblica / www.oblica.com.au
Tarlo & Graham / www.tarloandgraham.com
Temperature / www.temperaturedesign.com.au
Tigger Hall Design / www.tiggerhall.com
Vixen & Velvet / www.vixenandvelvet.com

USA
New York: Confetti System / www.confettisystem.com
Dosa / www.dosainc.com
Fredericks & Mae / www.fredericksandmae.myshopify.com
Love, Adorned / www.loveadorned.com
Mociun / www.mociun.com
Sri / www.srithreads.com
Philadelphia: Three Potato Four / www.threepotatofour.com
Los Angeles: General Store / www.shop-generalstore.com

OTHER
Japan: Analogue Life / www.analoguelife.com
Claska / www.claska.com
New Zealand: French Country / www.frenchcountry.co.nz
(through Julie Lewis Agency)
Belgium: Vincent van Duysen / www.vincentvanduysen.com
Ibiza: Sluiz / www.sluiz-ibiza.com
Netherlands: Piet Hein Eek / www.pietheineek.nl
Canada: Maiwa / www.maiwa.com
France: Porte De Clignancourt / www.marcheauxpuces-saintouen.com
Porte de Vanves flea market / www.pucesdevanves.typepad.com

Thank you

The wonderful Hannah, Leah, Leta, brother Chris, Georgie, Sal, Kelly & Jim for their ideas, enthusiasm, support and ability to make this book so much fun. My travel companions Dad, James Merrell, Mitzie & Chris who made my adventures what they were.

For all the places I shot at: Andrea & Robert of Byron View Farm, William & Jo of Fabulous Mrs Fox, the amazing team at Cockatoo Island, Glen Proebstel and Establishment Studios, La Casa Artist Residency, Peter Lewis and Christopher Boots.

Sean Cook for always having something lovely and in season, ABC Books, my travel agent Kim Mason for all her patience, the incredibly talented Racket who created all the maps throughout the book, and all the assistants who helped, organised, lifted, drove and contributed.

Published in 2014 by:
Harper Design
An Imprint of HarperCollins*Publishers*
10 East 53rd Street
New York, NY 10022
Tel (212) 207-7000
harperdesign@harpercollins.com
www.harpercollins.com

First published in Australia by:
HarperCollins*Publishers* Australia Pty Limited
harpercollins.com.au

Distributed in the United States and Canada by:
HarperCollins*Publishers*
10 East 53rd Street
New York, NY 10022

Styling and concept: Sibella Court
Art direction and design: Hannah Brady and Sibella Court
Editor: Leta Keens
Managing editor: Leah Rauch

Library of Congress Control Number: 2013944353

ISBN: 978-0-06-231833-6

Printed in China
First printing 2013